ABOUT THE AUTHOR

Vanessa Howard is a journalist and author. As a feature writer, she specialises in real life stories and has written for women's magazines, the press and broadcasters. Her non-fiction books have covered murder and reconciliation, unsolved UK murders and the psychology of female violence. She is married and has two children.

WOMEN
WHO KILL

Vanessa Howard

First published in 2010 by

Quercus
21 Bloomsbury Square
London
WC1A 2NS

A CIP catalogue record for this book is available
from the British Library

ISBN 978 1 84916 024 7

10 9 8 7 6 5 4 3 2 1

Typeset by Ellipsis Books Limited, Glasgow

Printed and bound in Great Britain by Clays Ltd, St Ives plc

To the women that strive to make a difference
and who never make the headlines.

ACKNOWLEDGEMENTS

I would like to thank the following for their help and support: Nick Scola, Graeme Gwyn, Willie Johnston, Lynne Vernon, Simon Barraclough, Mark Baker, Seamus Burke, Mick McCarron, Steve Arthur, Geoff Howard, Nick Johnston, Sarah Goodall, Neil Coyte, Karen Reeves, Cathie McGunnigle, Wensley Clarkson and David Howard.

CONTENTS

CHAPTER ONE

Chelsea O'Mahoney
The Happy Slapping Killer

A mob is the scum that rises upmost when the
nation boils

John Dryden

David Morley had known hatred. In some ways, his life had been buffeted by it but he refused to let it defeat his spirit. As a gay man, he'd known casual and derogatory abuse but by the late 1990s he felt that the worst might be over. It wasn't.

David was a bar manager in Soho, an area of central London that has long prided itself on its tolerance. It's cleaned up its act somewhat since its seedier image of the 1960s when it was synonymous with strip joints, drugs and prostitution. It is now dominated by bars and restaurants and attracts equal numbers of tourists and Londoners. There is a thriving gay scene, a number of bars and nightclubs that draw good crowds, something that another David, David Copeland, was aware of.

On 30 April 1999, Copeland travelled to central London from his rented room in Hampshire. His aim was simple. The Admiral Duncan on Old Compton Street in Soho was a gay-friendly pub and was to be his third target. He had, in the course of a few days, already detonated nail bombs on Electric Avenue in Brixton and Hanbury Street, close to Brick Lane. These were his terror attacks on London's black and Bangladeshi populations. Now he turned his attention to the gay community.

Copeland was a neo-Nazi and member of an organisation calling itself the National Socialist Movement. His aim was to stir up a race war and attack 'degenerates' for good measure. The bombs in Electric Avenue and Hanbury Street caused injuries but no fatalities but the bomb in the Admiral Duncan killed three customers: Andrea Dykes, out celebrating her pregnancy along with her husband Julian and two of their close friends. Of the group of four, only Julian Dykes survived.

The pub was a scene of devastation; four people would suffer amputations and close to eighty people were injured. David Morley was working behind the bar when the nail bomb exploded. He suffered burns to his head and hands but continued to help others before he was treated. After he recovered, he was told that the hearing loss to his left ear would be permanent but he worked tirelessly to reopen the bar, determined that an act of hate should not be allowed to triumph.

It was from Soho that he set out with a good friend, Alistair Whiteside, some five years later, walking for ten to fifteen minutes until they reached the South Bank. Set on the south side of the Thames, it is home to the Royal Festival Hall, Hayward Gallery and the London Eye and no matter the hour, this stretch of the river always seems to throng with activity – a perfect place, David and Alistair thought, to unwind after a busy night at work.

There has always been more than one London. There have always been the haves and have-nots, the law-abiding and the wrongdoers, those who seek to blend in and those who seek to stand out. The same land-scape, the same streets can be a safe metropolis to one man and a hunting ground for another. David Morley, survivor of one hate-fuelled act, was about to be targeted by another. Tragically, it would not be an attack he would walk away from.

A month prior to the night that David Morley's life was taken a fourteen-year-old girl wrote in her journal, *'Whats goin on I just come home yesterday I had an all nighter with Barry, Darren and Reece. It was Jokers or we went bare places. I was happy all night because Barry kept ramping all the time.'* Teenagers have long nurtured slang, creating and evolving it to ensure that they belong to one group and stand outside the adult world. Chelsea O'Mahoney was used to dividing one world from another, moving between the two when necessary, camouflaging what she truly felt at all times.

Even the diary entry wasn't an honest interrogation of what she thought, it was little more than an exercise in belonging. By talking through what she had participated in in the lingua franca of the group, she was playing with one aspect of her identity. Her teachers would not have recognised this 'Chelsea'. They believed she was a bright and creative young girl and were horrified to hear the journal's contents when they were presented at her trial. But Chelsea always needed to feel that she belonged and it was a longing that would have a deadly endgame.

'*Them lot bang up some old homeless man which I think was bad, which I think is bad but even though I was laughing though. Then we went back to Neeky's yard to cotch.*' David Morley had three weeks to live. As his life was narrowing to one point, so was Chelsea's. The night her gang decided to embark on an 'all nighter'. The night that she would participate in an hour-long rampage of violence. The night she would record their attacks on her mobile phone. It would not be her male counterparts that would adorn every newspaper, it would be her. Because, as a fourteen-year-old girl, she acted without mercy, without compassion and the judge

4

elected to remove restrictions on reporting details of her identity, even though she was a juvenile. He wanted it to be a wake-up call. How could a young girl take part in a vicious gang killing?

Her decline into lawlessness and violence didn't happen overnight. Chelsea may have reached a new level of notoriety because of her gender but her life story holds an all too common pattern of neglect and abuse suffered by too many boys and girls in the inner cities. She is one of an army of the neglected.

Chelsea Kayleigh Peaches O'Mahoney was born in a London hospital in the tail-end of a decade, on 15 November 1989. If the ethos of the 1980s centred on greed and gain Suzanne Cato, Chelsea's mother, was a casualty. She was a heroin addict who'd lost all contact with her parents. She drifted aimlessly and her relationships were short-lived, including that with Chelsea's father, believed to be another addict. Chelsea's birth certificate is blank where his name should appear.

Suzanne told social workers that she would stop abusing heroin and alcohol now that she was a mother. Her good intentions soon lay broken as the demands of mothering a newborn took hold. Suzanne returned to feeding her habit and Chelsea, like many other children of addicts, learnt that her needs would come a poor second.

It is difficult to calculate the impact an addict parent has on the life of the developing child. Early bonding and nurturing is vital in developing a child's mind, their responses to the world and to others. Neural pathways, the delicate interconnected areas of the brain, are forged through experience in the first few years. A child should live in an environment where it can associate needs with their fulfilment, pain with its relief and anxiety with comfort. Without this grounding, stress, want, hunger, fear and loneliness become the norm, ever-present and only inconsistently dealt with. It creates a toxic template, where anger is uncontrolled, feelings are volatile and the needs of others difficult to accommodate.

If the theory of child development seems obscure, the facts were plain. By three years old, Chelsea would watch as her mother injected heroin. She'd walk through discarded bottles of alcohol as she scavenged for food and she could be found to wander the streets alone, even at night. It would not take an expert to realise that here was a child whose life was in danger of being over even before it began.

Chelsea was not Suzanne's only child. She was already a mother of two but it must have been clear to social workers that she was not coping. By the age of seven, it was agreed that Chelsea would need to be placed elsewhere. The decision to take a child from a mother is never taken lightly and yet it has to remain an option. Chelsea was surviving, not developing, and the hope was that an aunt in south London might be able to provide her with the stability she craved.

There is something disquieting about the Jesuit maxim 'Give me the child until he is seven and I will show you the man'; it suggests that lives can be hard-wired to thrive or fail at a very young age. Whilst there are many examples of happy and successful people who began life as a deprived child, they tend to be the exceptions.

Chelsea's aunt was married and had no children of her own. When she agreed to foster her niece, it must have been with the hope that the first seven years of emotional damage could be repaired. The couple were not well-off but had passed the many requirements placed on them to foster. They were committed to raising her in a safe and caring environment and after a period of adjustment, Chelsea seemed to respond. Her teachers were positive about her progress, she was intelligent and enjoyed art in particular.

At home her behaviour was generally good although her aunt worried that she could switch off and withdraw emotionally if she felt pressured to communicate. This withdrawal was probably a mechanism she used when very young and with her mother still a factor in her life, the option to cut herself off was instinctive. Suzanne was allowed telephone contact but often failed to call or would speak to her when she was intoxicated. The impact on Chelsea could only be guessed at, but by age nine she asked for the calls to cease.

Although she was provided with a stable home life,

outside her front door there was another set of challenges to face. Sambrook House was one of a collection of low and high rises in Kennington which had fallen a long way short of the architects' post-war vision of clean, affordable community homes for blue-collar workers. Like many other high rises, they had fallen into a poor state of repair, with bored teens, graffiti and litter dominating the communal spaces. A lot of the flats were occupied by adults who had never worked and a culture of neglect and despair had become ingrained.

School was to be avoided or tolerated, a waiting time until it ended at sixteen and then life went on with no prospect of a job or further education. Crime was one route to a regular income of sorts but it was rarely organised at this level, it was merely another aspect of bullying and intimidation. Mobile phones were a typical example – they'd be ripped out of the hands of the more vulnerable or those who did not belong to a gang on the estate.

Whatever positive example was set at home, Chelsea found the allure of peer-group friendships too difficult to resist. Never having felt that she belonged, she was desperate not to be excluded. She was a follower, learnt the slang and the dress code and, increasingly, the attitude. Both her foster parents and teachers noted that she could have outbursts and use threatening language, perhaps in part by watching those she hung out with on the streets but undoubtedly in part because as she grew older, she was less inclined to have her behaviour checked.

She was developing a volatile personality. On one level she was able to read and write fluently, enjoy French lessons and send Christmas cards to teachers, and yet something would switch and the same girl would turn on teachers and use abusive language, would be disruptive and set out to upset her foster parents. Her aunt found it increasingly difficult to cope and asked for help. Family therapy was suggested and it was hoped that talking with Chelsea might help break the deadlock between them. It failed and her aunt asked that Chelsea be placed elsewhere.

This was in 2003 and Chelsea was thirteen years old. No matter the difficulties she'd found at home with her aunt and uncle, the request that she be moved on was a devastating blow. Chelsea may well have said that she was glad to be leaving but the emotional impact of another rejection was profound. She felt unwanted by the adult world and increasingly at home in her gang friendships, with their undercurrents of violence and petty crime.

Teenage gangs have come to haunt modern Britain. The hoodie, happy slapping, knife crime, reports of gang rapes where even girls have taken part, have all built an impression of sections of society sliding into barely contained lawlessness. The tabloid press have helped whip up a sense of despair but, crucially, it is not the readers who are ever likely to be victims. Most victims of teen-gang violence are other teenagers, usually from no more than a street or two away. The violence is, in the main, territorial, one block of flats setting out to attack the next.

The biggest impact teen-gang terror has is on its own neighbourhood. They dominate public spaces, like the communal greens that link high and low rises, and street corners, causing unease especially amongst the elderly. They create noise, vandalism, graffiti and litter and remain unchallenged, as law-abiding residents do not want to risk conflict and retribution. After all, these children will be neighbours.

Teenagers complain of boredom and a lack of facilities and see the streets as their only option. But it would take more than the opening of a youth club to untangle years of damage.

By fourteen years old, aggression as a means of survival has been hard-wired. Yet even then, gang dynamics are fluid and can remain as little more than a nuisance unless an 'initiator' joins the group. Then everything changes.

Camila Batmanghelidjh is the founder of Kids Company, the charity that works with traumatised and disadvantaged inner-city children. She has learnt that teen gangs are made up of imitators and initiators, and reveals: 'The initiator child sets the temperature at street level, influencing the behaviour of imitator children …

Imitator children are bullied, or watch their peers being deeply humiliated. They are forced into imitating violence to acquire a higher power rating.'

It is easy to imagine. The most volatile member of the gang shifts behaviour to extremes leaving others to either follow or become the object of derision and potentially, even a victim. As an initiator, David Blenman could have walked out of Central Casting.

Chelsea met Blenman once she was moved away from her foster parents and into the flat of another aunt and another high rise in Kennington. Blenman had never known his father and any care he received was sporadic. In the main he was brought up by an aunt and a grandmother but was known to be disruptive and violent by the time he started school. His attendance in school was poor, and perhaps in desperation he was sent to live with relatives in Barbados for a spell of his childhood. When he returned, no doubt with deep feelings of resentment at having been passed from one set of relatives to another, his behaviour was worse than ever.

He built up a long list of convictions, many for petty crime and affray. Even though he was younger, at fifteen, he dominated the older members of the group such as Darren Case and Reece Sargeant. Chelsea was the lynch pin and had got to know them whilst living on the separate estates. They would come together either to play football on disused ground or to drink and plan their 'ramping', or street robberies.

Chelsea did not stay with the second aunt for long. She became ill and her niece was effectively made homeless. In time, a new set of foster parents were found for her in South Norwood, about seven miles south of Kennington. Her new foster parents had children of their own and had fostered before with positive results. They were also selected as their address meant that Chelsea did not have to move school. At first, her behaviour seemed to improve and her foster parents were able to curb any rudeness she indulged in whilst at school. Outside the classroom, Chelsea chose to stay part of her gang and even had a brief relationship with Blenman.

It is probable that no matter how fair-minded her new foster parents were, it would take a long time before Chelsea could develop trust and the confidence that she would not be moved along once more. They told her that they were happy for her to stay until she reached eighteen and she was given certain freedoms, such as meeting up with her old friends at the weekend and even staying out overnight at a girlfriend's house. But Chelsea lied about where she was staying – she was, in fact, running with the gang as part of their 'all-nighters'.

This involved moving outside the Kennington estates and wandering closer into central London. It was a much easier hunting ground as even the most streetwise Londoner has their guard down in well-lit and busy streets. They would snatch mobile phones, ambush people by kicking and punching them to the ground, and Chelsea took to filming the attacks. It would allow the group to revisit the incidents later, a source of high amusement.

These random and cruel acts had an important role to play in the group. It elevated them into a sense of invulnerability and control. They may have been terrorised as children, have known violence and degradation but now, physically stronger, they could mete out their own humiliation. They were the ones to be feared now.

Violence can bond a group but it also works on an individual level and perhaps in the most surprising way of all. Camila Batmanghelidjh has spent many hours with young and violent offenders. She was told what it felt like to harm someone: 'They experience calm after battering someone.'

If they are reminded of their former vulnerability, they feel a rage they cannot channel or diffuse. After inflicting pain and distress on someone, they can experience a neurochemical release that is soothing. It is a disturbing inversion of normal behaviour. In children from stable and caring homes, empathy with others is reinforced over years. To use extreme physical aggression, this child would need to feel very threatened, triggering the 'fight or flight' syndrome. The body is flooded with adrenalin and the chemical after-effects of a violent episode are unpleasant, invoking shaking and nausea. But for the damaged child, it offers relief.

Today, clinical psychologists are questioning old assumptions that girls process anger differently from boys. It was believed that girls internalise pain, expressing it in episodes of self-harm. Whilst it is true that incidents of cutting and anorexia are higher amongst girls, it is also true that female violence is on the rise. Venting rage by attacking others was thought of as almost exclusively male behaviour, but no longer.

Just over fifty years ago, men would commit eleven offences for every one carried out by a woman. That figure has now narrowed to four-to-one. In addition, if girls were caught breaking the law, it was most likely to be for shoplifting, but violent crimes committed by women have doubled since the millennium. To put that in context, the police have complained of being overstretched as they arrest, on average, 240 women every day for violent offences in England and Wales.

The picture is no better in Scotland; the rise in female violence is UK-wide. The Scottish Lord Advocate, Elish Angiolini, spelt out what the change in statistics and behaviour means: 'They are not just going along with a dominant male partner, being an accessory, carrying knifes for boyfriends, assisting in cleaning up after a murder, hiding weapons, but are prime movers.'

Girls are integrated into teen gangs, they expect to take part, not watch from the sidelines. And so when

Chelsea left her neat bedroom in South Norwood on 29 October 2004, it would not be to act as a brake to the horror that would unfold, it would not be to intervene or ask her friends to stop. It would be to enjoy it to the full.

Blenman was bored. He was bored of Kennington and wanted to get into South Bank and bring his brand of group terror to anyone unfortunate enough to catch his eye. He set off with five others in tow.

CCTV cameras are now part of the landscape in our towns, passively recording the movements of passers-by. There are thousands of cameras in London, each stockpiling images, the majority unmanned and only accessed if the police are searching for footage of a potential crime. When the police began the time-consuming task of retrieving images of the early hours of 30 October, they had little idea that they would trace fifty minutes of terror.

David Dobson, a 24-year-old actor, had been working a shift at the bar of the Old Vic theatre. He left work a little before two thirty a.m. and headed left into Lower Marsh street, making his way home. He saw Chelsea and her friends, most with their hoods up, stretched out across the road ahead of him. The tallest sauntered over to him and asked: 'Have you got the time?' It was a signal and before Mr Dobson could answer, he'd been punched hard in the face. He was lucky. He'd fallen to the ground and was kicked repeatedly but managed to scramble to his feet and run.

The group did not chase him. In fact, in perhaps the most remarkable detail of the minutes that follow, over the course of eight assaults, the group did not run once. They attacked and simply strolled away, chatting as if nothing had happened, even though their bloodlust was high.

Turning towards the river, they came across David Morley and Alistair Whiteside sitting on a bench next to Hungerford Bridge. Chelsea walked over to them, a smile on her face. She held up a camera phone and said: 'We're doing a documentary on happy slapping. Pose for the camera.' At that, both men were pulled from the bench and savagely beaten. David Morley bore the brunt of the attack; Alistair Whiteside turned to see his friend being jumped and stamped on.

Five ribs were broken, his spleen ruptured and a pathologist would later count forty-four separate injuries. He likened the severity of his injuries to those seen on car crash victims or on someone who'd fallen from a great height. All inflicted by the fists and feet of teenagers. As the attack subsided, Chelsea picked up the bags and belongings of the two men. But that was not all. She took a step back and kicked David Morley's head, as Alistair Whiteside would later testify, 'like a footballer taking a penalty'. She walked quietly away to rejoin the group, and as she checked her phone, David Morley's life bled away.

Like a hideous pastiche of tourists taking in the sights, the gang then ambled towards the London Eye. The night was far from over. They then came across three foreign exchange students, sitting chatting together. All three were attacked, one had his mobile phone taken and a beer bottle was taken from another. Again, the students were lucky that the attack was brief and the gang turned their attention to walking towards Jubilee Gardens.

Nigel Elliot had missed his train. Waterloo Station was moments away but he had decided to gather his thoughts after a night out by sitting on a bench close to the London Eye. The bottle taken from the student moments earlier was smashed down over Mr Elliot's head. His pockets were searched and as he managed to get to his feet and tried to run, he was tripped up and repeatedly kicked in the face by at least two attackers. Then it was silent. The gang simply wandered away.

The last attack of the night would be played in court some months later, to shocked silence. Wayne Miller was sleeping in an underpass; homeless, he was at least not at risk from rain. At around three thirty a.m., he heard voices approach and then felt the first kick to his back. Picked up in the CCTV footage are Reece Sargeant, David Blenman and Darren Case. Standing behind them is Chelsea, her arm aloft holding a camera phone.

The attack takes only a few minutes but in that brief space of time, the prone and defenceless Wayne Miller is stamped on, kicked and punched. At one point, one of his attackers is seen to rest both hands against the wall. This allows him to jump on Mr Miller with both feet.

Such savagery is difficult to watch – even the experienced police officers who scanned to footage were appalled. But there was one witness who didn't flinch, one who watched and calmly filmed a man who was beaten mercilessly.

Wayne Miller was lucky to escape serious and permanent injury. Once more, the group calmly walked away and decided to make their way back to Kennington.

They went back to the estate to enjoy reminiscing about the night, replay the footage of their savagery and laugh as they heard their victims plead. As they whiled away the early hours, David Morley was in surgery at St Thomas's Hospital. Chelsea and her friends knew the hospital well as they played football in the waste ground that borders it. Surgeons struggled to repair David Morley's damaged internal organs but in vain. He died from of a haemorrhage from his ruptured spleen whilst in intensive care.

As the group hung out together, they looked at their spoils of the evening: mobile phones taken from one of the French students and from Alistair Whiteside. Reece Sargeant called his girlfriend just after four a.m. on the morning of the attacks. He boasted that he was calling her from a stolen mobile phone. Calls were made from Alistair Whiteside's phone also, all of which would prove vital when the police pieced together the events that had led to eight people being assaulted and one fatality.

At first, the police were not sure if they were dealing with a homophobic attack or if the group chose who to assault for no other reason than the fact that they crossed their path. As David Morley had already been caught up in one hate-crime, they looked closely for evidence that the teenagers had been motivated by homophobia.

What they would uncover was a hatred of a different kind. It did not discriminate and it was as volatile and as chaotic as the lives of the perpetrators. These children did not see their victims as human beings, they saw them only as a target for their rage and their pleas for mercy merely egged them on.

As Camila Batmanghelidjh has learnt: 'If the victim pleads, the perpetrator's response is one of revulsion: they don't like begging because it reminds them of when they were children, pleading but with no one to protect them.'

But these were no master criminals. Police were quickly able to establish a list of names, their addresses and their whereabouts. The mobile phone calls only added to the impression that they lacked understanding of the enormity of their crime. One fifteen-year-old friend of Chelsea's told the police that she'd listened as the group talked about its plans to target 'tramps, druggies or just people on the street' only two days before the attack and how they would divide up any spoils from the robberies.

On 8 November, just a week after David Morley's death, the police were at the door of Chelsea's foster parents' home. They saw Chelsea enter the house with a blue bag and she blurted out to officers: 'That's what I wore on the night.' They found her diaries, the entries written in street language all about previous attacks and her feelings about them, writing that they were 'bad' but that she still found herself laughing along. The two sides of Chelsea O'Mahoney, the bright and thoughtful girl being overruled by the callous and aggressive side that had allowed her to survive.

Under police questioning, Chelsea boxed clever, belying her fourteen years. She was not a veteran when it came to time spent in police stations, unlike David Blenman, so her performance was all the more extraordinary. She probed what the police knew, asking of the attack on David Morley: 'But don't you have CCTV footage from where it happened?' She changed tack several times, sometimes blocking by simply saying she couldn't remember her computer password, at other times trying to put forward excuses, suggesting that she wasn't using her phone and was just looking through the phonebook on her friend's mobile, not filming the attack.

She'd wiped her phone. The police tried to rebuild the footage taken and texts sent but it proved impossible. Chelsea knew that CCTV was a possibility but knew she'd deleted her phone files. She was weighing up the chance of walking away from a charge.

Perhaps she could play the role of innocent spectator? When asked why she hadn't left the gang she said: 'What was I supposed to do? Now if I'd tried to stop them, what if they'd like, what if they'd have turned on me like, what was I supposed to do?' It was a valid question although the detective questioning her soon demolished her attempt to suggest she was too terrified to act or to run away. He asked: '... when someone is getting the hiding of their lives, it's not the normal actions of a person to scroll through a friend's phone, is it?'

It isn't, but Chelsea and her friends were far from 'normal'. Their sense of right and wrong was so corrupt, David Morley stood no chance. Chelsea took aim at his head, like a footballer taking a penalty, knowing that her audience of boy-gang members were watching and she knew that she could not miss.

In January 2006, Sargeant, Case and Blenman were each given twelve-year sentences and Chelsea eight years for the manslaughter of David Morley. She knew what was on the cards and had lapsed into her violent persona to survive being held on remand at Oakhill secure unit. What she had not expected was to be named and shamed by the judge, as she was still a minor.

The judge, Brian Barker, did so to highlight the nature of crime emerging from lives such as Chelsea's, a life he described as 'particularly chaotic and fragmented'. But no matter the hardship faced in childhood, Mr Barker had no hesitation in stating this could never excuse what they did. 'You are all old enough to understand the realities and the consequences of your actions,' he said. 'You sought enjoyment from humiliation and pleasure from the infliction of pain.'

Two worlds came together in the early hours of 31 October. David Morley, who gave away much of the compensation money he received after surviving the Admiral Duncan bombing to charities, and Chelsea O'Mahoney, just one of many young girls born to a generation blighted by drug addiction and urban decay.

That is why her case caused such consternation, not because she was unique but that she is just one of the many abandoned and violent children that stalk the inner cities.

It wasn't the first time two worlds collided on the streets of the nation's capital and it won't be the last. When they meet, it reveals just how dangerous the gulf is. On the day of the verdict, David Morley's family had to watch as some of the defendant's family and friends screamed abuse at them. One man even drew a finger across his throat.

Violence is a virus, and it spreads fastest amongst children. Chelsea O'Mahoney may be the first girl we remember being labelled as a gang-killer but she will be joined by others.

CHAPTER TWO

Heather Stephenson-Snell
Therapist Turned Stalker

In jealousy there is more self-love than love
François VI, Duc de La Rochefoucauld

In the early hours of 1 November 2003, traffic police on the M62 began to follow a red G-registered Ford Escort driving in the slow lane. It was a little after one thirty a.m. and, at a guess, the driver had probably had too much to drink. Not because she was driving recklessly, rather the opposite and just as sure a giveaway; she was driving too slowly.

The car was flagged over to the hard shoulder and the police officer knocked on the driver's side window. A woman wound down the window and addressed the officer. She wasn't drunk, she spoke clearly and held the officer's gaze but she had clear bruising across her eye and left cheek. Beyond that, she looked middle-aged and professional as she quietly gave her name and explained that she was driving back to her home in York. The name would turn out to be false. As the officer was taking down her details, something in the footwell of the back seat caught his eye. It was a white robe and it looked stained.

He asked the driver to step out of the car and the officer walked to the back door and opened it. He picked up a white sheet and found a sawn-off shotgun and cartridges. As he guessed, the garment he'd picked up was stained, but until that moment he would not have believed it was real, not fake blood. Placed under arrest for possession of a firearm, the woman was then frisked and a knife was pulled from her waistband. It had been a routine traffic stop but without realising it the officer had arrested one of the most bizarre and extraordinary of modern female killers.

Very little of what Greater Manchester Police were told by the woman over the following hours and days would turn out to be reliable. Presented with facts, she quickly and seamlessly changed tack. She appeared unconcerned when questioned and the only issue that animated her concerned food – she refused to eat anything but bagels.

The police established that the car she was driving had been recently bought and was registered to a Ms Heather Stephenson-Snell. At the time of her arrest, she was wearing men's clothes and it wasn't clear who they belonged to. Her address was traced and 137 Crombie Avenue, York turned out not only to be her home but her work premises. Stephenson-Snell was a registered counsellor and psychotherapist who specialised in art therapy. 'I am a very creative person,' she would say.

Ms Stephenson-Snell had a very high opinion of her talents and her intelligence and did little to cooperate with the police. Yet in the end, her cooperation wasn't needed as she was so highly organised that she had detailed her murder plan on neatly filed index cards. It revealed exactly how she planned to murder Diane Lomax. Yet it wasn't Lomax who lay brutally shot dead on a pavement in Radcliffe, near Bury.

Bob Wilkie knew how to handle himself. An ex-Marine Commando, he may no longer have been in the kind of shape that he was in his twenties but even at 43 years old he had the kind of bulky physical presence that lent him confidence. In 2003, his life seemed to be turning around. At the start of the year he'd met 40-year-old Debbie O'Brien and to his surprise, they had found love. She had two young children from a previous relationship and Bob soon won their trust and affection. By the autumn, Bob asked Debbie to marry him and, ever the old-fashioned gent, he'd even asked her father's permission first. Debbie said yes and the couple were living together at her home in Holland Street, Radcliffe.

Debbie had done a lot for Bob in their short time together. He'd spoken about his older brother Billy and his regret that they had fallen out over something minor some years before. With Debbie's encouragement, Bob picked up the phone and the two brothers were reconciled. Blood is thicker than water and the 47-year-old Billy realised how much he'd missed his younger brother as the years had passed. He was delighted to hear of Bob's wedding plans and it meant a lot to know that he'd be there to witness them tie the knot.

Two weeks later, it was Hallowe'en and Debbie and Bob hoped the evening wouldn't be too hectic. Over the years, Hallowe'en had completely changed in character, importing a few traditions from the US to become an altogether bigger undertaking than it ever had been growing up in the 1970s and 80s. Trick or treating was a growth pastime and households were now having to remember to stock bowls of sweets and chocolates for the children that would knock on the door.

Bob wasn't enamoured with the way Hallowe'en had changed. He didn't mind the primary school children that dressed up in their costumes coming knocking with a parent, but for teenagers, the last night of October was often an excuse for mischief. He was concerned for older residents, many of whom found the use of masks and hoodies nothing less than intimidating. It got dark early at this time of year and even at five thirty p.m.

the crowds of teens at bus stops and street corners were already wearing their disguises.

The 'Scream' masks were the worst. Some of the ghoulish disguises were cartoon-like but they'd often be passed over for the mask inspired by the 1996 hit film *Scream*. Although a Wes Craven spoof on 'slasher' films like *Halloween*, it still contained a number of bloodthirsty murders, all carried out by a teenage boy and his accomplice wearing the Scream mask. The face looks like the tormented soul represented in Edvard Munch's painting *The Scream*, but for nearly all under-twenties it means little more than the scary new slasher-hit franchise, now on its fourth instalment. Did Heather Stephenson-Snell, by then forty-five years old, know that? Dressed in male clothes, with the mask on, she looked like a teenage boy.

That was the sight that confronted Bob Wilkie just after midnight on Hallowe'en. The night had passed off relatively peacefully and Debbie and the children were asleep. Holland Road is a quiet street of modest terraced houses tightly packed together. A car had pulled up and managed to find a parking spot – quite a stroke of luck as it was not always guaranteed. The driver got out of the car, marched up to the house next to Debbie O'Brien's home and began to hammer on the door. No one answered. The banging went on and Debbie was worried the noise would wake her children, if not the whole street.

She was sure that there was someone in next door; Diane Lomax and Adrian Sinclair, a couple of a similar age, lived there. The knocking went on and on and Bob had had enough. It may have been Saturday the next morning but that was no excuse to disturb everyone's sleep. Wearing only a pair of boxer shorts, Bob pulled open his door and confronted the person who was causing mayhem. As he stood on the doorstep, the figure turned to him. It unnerved him to see a figure wearing a mask. Bob asked what they thought they were playing at and told them to go home. 'Mind your own business,' said a voice from within the mask. But this was his business and Bob would not be so easily intimidated.

Let's see how brave this character is when they are not hiding behind a disguise, he thought. He asked them to remove the mask, the figure told him to get back inside, Bob didn't. He took another step forward and pulled off the mask. It was to be his last action. From under the white gown there was a crack of gunfire. The noise was deafening and Diane Lomax finally opened her door. She glanced outside, screamed and slammed it closed again. Later in court, CCTV footage had not picked up the shooting, but it had recorded sound. The sound of a door being hammered, the sound of voices and then the loud and single shot as Bob Wilkie was blasted at point-blank range.

Bob flew backwards and hit the ground – he'd been shot in the torso. On the tape, female voices can be heard screaming, Bob's name is called out. A neighbour called 999 but even though an ambulance was on the scene in minutes, there was nothing that could be done to save Bob Wilkie.

The masked figure was nowhere to be seen. After discharging the firearm, the weapon's recoil had forced the barrel to smash backwards and it would leave heavy facial bruising around the cheek and left eye. Yet the killer had the presence of mind to calmly walk back to the parked Ford Escort and drive away. The mask was left on Bob's doorstep. None of it made sense.

Just over an hour later, Heather Stephenson-Snell was pulled over by West Yorkshire Police for driving too slowly on the M62, heading towards York. She was on her way home, that much was true. When her movements of that evening were pieced together, the police were staggered. What on earth would make a 45-year-old therapist dress up on Hallowe'en and murder an innocent bystander? The reason, when it emerged, was more bizarre than anyone could have imagined.

The press had a field day. Here was a respectable middle-aged professional who'd hatched a murderous plan to avenge herself on her ex-boyfriend. The target was not Bob Wilkie. It was Diane Lomax, the current girlfriend of Stephenson-Snell's former boyfriend, Adrian Sinclair. There is a much-used saying that hell hath no fury like a woman scorned, but this was no ordinary 'crime of passion'. The more the press dug, the more incredible Stephenson-Snell's life appeared. By the time of her trial for murder and attempted murder at Manchester Crown Court in 2004, this would be a tale of an all-girl biker gang, a former male stripper, pornography, stalking and mental illness. A split life spiralling away from reality and coalescing around a single fantasy and one night of murder.

Understanding how the situation came about requires more than piecing together the facts as they are known, it requires the kind of detective work Heather would have appreciated and understood – psychological analysis. It is paradoxical to use the techniques Heather was familiar with, but failed so wholly to use to heal herself, but without them her actions remain inexplicable.

Heather Stephenson was born in 1957 in Malta, where her father was a serving soldier in the British Army. She learnt early that as an 'army brat', home would not remain home for long. A rootless existence suits some but not all and many other children who grew up with parents in the Army have complained that it can be difficult to form attachments to a place or a community when the next posting could be any time soon. It isn't unknown for them to have been pushed through eight or more schools by the time they are sixteen. For Heather, however, there was an added complication. Her parents' marriage was in trouble and by the age of seven, it had broken down completely.

Her mother decided against coming back to the UK and instead moved herself, Heather and her brother to Canada. They would stay there for the next six years but again, her mother found it hard to settle and she knew the move would not be a permanent one. They would return to the UK in the end. At first, aged thirteen, Heather was sent to a boarding school in Kent but she hated it. It was a difficult age, hitting puberty with no clear sense of who she was or where she belonged. An outsider in Canada for being too English, she was now an outsider in England for her weird-sounding accent.

Her next move was to the other end of the country, up north to the Yorkshire seaside town of Scarborough. There, she would live with an aunt, a difficult time as her relationship with her mother had broken down, and her father had no role to play in her life. Heather still had much in her favour, she was a bright and capable student but she took no solace in schoolwork. She began to make up stories to try and impress school mates, sometimes telling people that her father was a spy, at other times claiming that he was a famous author. She was old enough to know better but it was part of her compulsive need to be taken notice of and to be seen as special.

If she had poured as much energy into schoolwork, she could have achieved good academic grades and that would have acted as a springboard out of her life in

Scarborough. But she limped through to sixteen years old with only a few CSEs to her name. Heather was drifting and her life was to take a turn for the worst.

Her late teens would be marred by run-ins with the police over a string of minor offences, petty theft and criminal damage. She was drinking and, after several appearances before magistrates, it seemed that Heather was on track for a custodial sentence and descent into a life of petty crime. But then she met Leo Snell.

He ran a bookshop and hired Heather to work alongside him. Heather could charm when she chose to and before long the two were an item. Within months, they had married and had planned a move to the pretty and prosperous town of Penrith, on the edge of the Lake District. By the time she was twenty-one, Heather was married and mother to a son they called Solomon. It should have been a fresh start, the chance to draw a line under all her adolescent unhappiness and create the kind of home life that she had sought but that had always eluded her. But it wasn't to be. Her marriage was soon in trouble and history seemed to be repeating itself. Like his mother, Solomon would reach his seventh birthday and face the realities of life with parents who had separated acrimoniously.

But Heather chose not to leave Penrith, at least not initially. She enrolled on a Social Sciences course through the Open University and she thrived. She had an aptitude for study after all, and was determined to make something of her life. By 1987, aged thirty, she had gained a place at York University as a mature student studying psychology. Again, if this were fiction, it would have been a turning point. But Heather's life was far from straightforward and the year before she took up her place at York, she was once again in trouble with the police and faced charges of theft and criminal damage.

Heather was no longer a troubled youth but an adult, and this should have acted as a clear warning that hers was a complex personality. Achieving academic success and the veneer of respectability on one hand, whilst at the same time acting on destructive impulses and breaking the law. Who was the real Heather?

York University in the late 1980s was described somewhat tongue-in-cheek as a 'nice campus, in a nice town, with nice courses and nice students'. Predominantly middle-class, students were academic high achievers and studious. The Quaker ethos was alive and well on the close-knit campus. As a mature student, Heather would have been off the radar for the majority of the students – being thirty would have been seen as practically middle-aged. The psychology department was on the outskirts of the campus too so there was another element of isolation that she would have to overcome. Once more, Heather was an outsider.

The course was prestigious but as Heather was studying for a Batchelor of Science degree, it was also firmly laboratory based. This was a science degree, not the humanities degree which would incorporate the softer communication and counselling skills that would later attract her. Graduating in 1990, Heather would remain in the city, not because of any firm attachment to a career or relationship but because she was unsure of what to do next.

Heather would not be caught breaking the law again until the catastrophic events of thirteen years later, and although she would pour her efforts into building a viable business as a counsellor, other darker aspects of her personality would still play themselves out. She had a fascination with weapons and began collecting knives, replica guns and machetes. She joined a women's bikers' club and would attend rallies, eventually rising to head one chapter of a group in York. She drank heavily and would use recreational drugs, all activities that were in marked contrast to her daytime persona; a woman who wore conservative suits and set out to counsel others suffering with depression or addictive behaviour.

Working for herself suited Heather. Financially, she would never earn more than a moderate wage and by 2000 it made economic sense to move her practice, York Psychotherapy Clinic, to her home in Crombie Avenue, a modest street of post-war housing and small businesses, about a mile and a half from the city centre. There she registered with the National Council of Psychotherapists, an organisation of mainly self-employed practitioners that offer everything from help with stress to 'past-life regression' and help to quit smoking.

Without doubt, 'personal growth' has been a boom industry over the last twenty years. Every possible therapy is now available to the public from Meridian Therapy to Chakra Balancing, Crystal Reiki and Hopi Ear Candling. Traditional medicine may view the treatments with a degree of scepticism yet it has not prevented the rise of complementary therapies. It can be argued that many of the treatments have little discernible medical benefit but word-of-mouth reports of 'cures' for long-standing complaints have ensured that alternative therapies continue to thrive.

Into this blurring of conventional and non-conventional treatments stepped Heather Stephenson-Snell. Unlike many practitioners in arts that offer a 'realignment of the body's energy system', Heather did have a degree in psychology but her degree was based on the experimental analysis of human behaviour – for example studying how language is acquired – and should not be confused with therapy, mysticism and self-discovery. Psychology graduates are just as likely to embark on a career in market research as they are to consider psychotherapy, a wholly different field. Psychotherapy, or 'talking therapies' requires separate specialist training.

Patients feel confident if they can see certificates on

the wall and Heather projected a professional manner, perfectly able to talk at length about different treatments and routes to attaining a change in patient behaviour. Indeed, she wrote and published several articles, for example questioning the role of psychometric testing within counselling. She wrote confidently about testing techniques such as the Beck Hopelessness Scale and the Rust Inventory of Schizotypal Cognitions but never, it seems, turning much of her insight and technique onto her own troubled inner life.

By the time she met Adrian Sinclair, early in 2002, the different and opposing parts of her personality were set to pull her mental health apart. Not that Adrian saw that at first – few did. He had answered an advertisement in the *Big Issue* from a woman looking for a dog sitter. Knocking at the door in Crombie Avenue, Adrian was met by the professional and well-heeled Heather. She explained that although she had only been in Crombie Avenue for a couple of years, she had run her successful practice for over a decade. She had two well-kept Rottweilers and offered him the job of a 'live-in' sitter. Adrian's role was to walk and care for the dogs during the day whilst Heather attended to her patients' needs.

Frankly, Adrian needed the work. He had a number of casual jobs but little that was permanent; he'd even had stints working as a stripper but it wasn't a role he enjoyed. He was honest about his past and told Heather that he'd had his share of troubles but that he now hoped to be a writer, and Heather seemed a very sympathetic listener. She was a creative person too, she told him, and was interested in exploring more creative writing herself. Adrian hoped the house on Crombie Avenue would prove the ideal setting, providing a roof over his head, steady employment and the opportunity to write. Heather seemed pleasant and genuinely interested in him.

And indeed she was. Within a couple of weeks they had embarked on a sexual relationship and Adrian learnt more than he ever bargained for. Heather showed him her weapon collection. She showed him the 'den' she'd created in her garage, somewhere she called the Orange Pit and the venue for drink and drug parties she'd host for her biker friends. She boasted about the attacks she'd carried out on people who crossed her, stating that few who got in her way remained unscathed. There was definitely a wild side to Heather, Adrian thought.

She poured her attention onto him at first. She quizzed him about his early life and he opened up to her. Everything between them developed at a breakneck rate but began to deteriorate with equal speed. When it turned sour it did so overnight, with Heather deciding that Adrian was not suitable to look after her dogs. She also announced that she'd be going on an extended creative writing course in New York for three months, and it was clear that he was no longer welcome; yet when she left, Adrian was still staying at Crombie Avenue and had no plans to move. Only when she left did he move out and find somewhere to rent, in Radcliffe on the outskirts of Manchester.

Heather found out and, rather than being relieved, she was enraged. She began calling Adrian from New York, leaving sexually explicit messages. She then found out that not only had he moved away, he'd started an affair with someone new; Diane Lomax. This was the tipping point. Instead of retreating, Heather launched a campaign against the couple that only ended with murder the following year.

It began with abusive messages. Heather had taken Adrian's address book before she left for New York and began calling his friends and family and either making bizarre accusations or acting as the wounded party. Adrian was the focus for much of her anger. She would switch from provocative and sexual letters and calls to outright threats. This was classic stalking behaviour.

Psychiatrists Dr David James, Dr Frank Farnham and Dr Paul Cantrell from the Royal Free and University College Medical School in North London, carried out a study in 2000 that noted that if the stalker had a previous sexual relationship with their victim, there was a 70 per cent likelihood that they would attempt to seriously injure their target. But in Heather's mind, the target was shifting.

After she arrived back from New York, Heather became fixated on Diane and Adrian. Heather would call Diane and leave abusive messages, calling her rival a 'slag' and a 'prostitute'. Adrian somewhat foolishly agreed to call at Crombie Avenue to talk to Heather. If that was a naïve move, his next was reckless. They had sex. The next morning, Adrian left hastily and regretted his behaviour but there can be little doubt that in Heather's mind a link between the two had been reforged. That he had elected to leave, to return to Diane, meant that Diane was now the obstacle. Someone as smart as Heather was used to overcoming obstacles.

What followed was a frightening escalation in Heather's campaign of harassment. She would call them ten times or more a day, it was clear that she had been watching the couple, and what worried Diane most was Heather's references to her walking her two children to school. They contacted the police but beyond issuing some general advice about keeping a log of the incidents, the couple felt they were not taken seriously.

Taking matters into his own hands, Adrian decided they should relocate from Radcliffe to Huddersfield, some thirty miles away. As they unpacked, the phone rang. It was Heather. She asked: 'What's the weather like in Huddersfield?'

Photographs arrived at the house. Some showed

Adrian with a woman's face scratched out, others showed Diane with her children. The threat was clear and Heather even went as far as stating she would cut off her rival's breasts. It seems extraordinary that a working psychotherapist could behave in such a way, demonstrating all the disturbed behaviour of a case study in dysfunction, and yet although women are in a minority when it comes to stalking, research suggests that they tend to be people with higher than average intelligence. Clearly, being bright didn't cause Heather to pause and reflect on her behaviour, it merely allowed her to plan her hateful campaign more meticulously.

She informed social services that Diane was abusing her children – as a professional, she would have known that she was not required to leave her details with the authorities. Social services accept anonymous tip-offs as they are aware that some neighbours or family members will be reluctant to speak out otherwise. But that allows the system to be misused by malicious individuals, leaving a family with sickening allegations to refute. Heather, in the meantime, sat back and watched the drama unfold.

Female stalkers are rare but they do account for about 15 per cent of cases and alarmingly are just as likely to attack their victims as men. As professor of forensic psychiatry Paul Mullen states: 'There is no reason to presume that the impact of being stalked by a female would be any less devastating than that of a man.' The one notable difference between Heather's behaviour and that of the other female stalkers in Professor Mullen's 2002 research paper was that women often pursue people they had professional contact with, especially psychiatrists, psychologists and doctors. Heather was remarkable as here the situation appeared in reverse – the therapist as stalker.

Heather's professional role makes her case highly unusual but she is far from alone as a woman intent on a bloody revenge. She has refused to talk about what motivated her murderous campaign but it is in another recent case that we can gain some insight.

When Rena Salmon's marriage broke down after eighteen years, she learned to her dismay that it was because her husband, Paul, had begun an affair with her best friend, Lorna Stewart. Lorna ran a beauty salon in Chiswick, west London, and when Rena found out that the couple planned to have children, something snapped.

The 43-year-old mother of two drove to Chiswick from her home in Great Shefford, Berkshire, armed with a double-barrelled shotgun and fired twice at her love rival, at close range. Lorna was two months pregnant at the time of her death. Moments after the shooting, Rena dialled 999 and said: 'I have shot my husband's mistress.' She was jailed for life in 2003.

In an attempt to explain her catastrophic loss of

control, Rena said that she intended to kill herself, not Lorna. The jury did not believe her, nor were they swayed by mitigating circumstances introduced at her trial to explain her mental collapse. Yet Rena Salmon's case is valuable as it reveals what can elevate a jealous rage into cold-blooded murder.

Despite the outward appearance as a happy and affluent full-time mum, Rena claims she was tormented by insecurities from childhood. Of mixed race, Rena said that her mother had scrubbed her skin with bleach, a claim her mother denied. She also denied Rena's accusation that she brought a string of lovers into the family home. Whatever the truth behind the claims, Rena's relationship with her mother was volatile and she ran away from home aged thirteen. She was placed in foster care and joined the army six years later; when serving in Northern Ireland, she met her future husband, Paul.

Fearing that the stable home life she had always sought was now destroyed, Rena believed that all was lost, and in a state of desperation her mind snapped. It cannot be without significance that the day she got into her car with the shotgun was the evening before her divorce would become final.

An unstable and unhappy background does seem to have a part to play in the lives of women that become stalkers and women who plan violent assaults against a 'rival'. In an oddly light-heartedly titled research paper called 'These Boots Are Made For Stalking', Dr Sara West and Dr Susan Friedman discovered that there appears to be a high rate of sexual (45 per cent) and physical (30 per cent) abuse in the personal histories of the female stalkers. This in turn could trigger the borderline personality or post-traumatic stress disorders.

Rena Salmon would recognise the toxic mix of emotions Dr West and Dr Friedman list as drivers for stalking, including anger, obsession, feelings of abandonment, loneliness, and dependency. Whilst Heather has remained silent on the subject of her childhood, her behaviour was revealing.

In the first instance, there is a lot to be learnt from the way she expressed her fantasy life. There is evidence that early in adolescence, Heather was capable of lying to increase her sense of importance and to gain centre stage. Clearly, she needed others to see her as a significant personality, probably the result of feeling conditionally out of place both at home and in the number of different towns and communities in which she lived in her early years.

Unlike Rena, however, Heather did not seem cowed and insecure about her childhood. Articulate and confident, she was able to charm others and never doubted that she was intelligent. Yet with the episodes of petty theft and minor offences, Heather had difficulty in controlling her impulses. She would have known the difference between right and wrong as a teen yet was still offending in her late twenties. What she failed to do was turn her intelligence in on herself to examine why she would break the law, what was driving her antisocial behaviour?

Rather than trying to understand why, Heather may well have simply learnt not to get caught. There is no evidence that she broke the law after her last court appearance in 1986 but she spoke frequently to Adrian about attacking those who had 'crossed her'. This may have been fantasy but it is just as revealing. Heather reached adulthood imagining that she was smarter than others, capable of avenging slights, and boosted her sense of potency with the usual paraphernalia of knives, guns, and, it can even be argued, 'macho' dogs in her choice of Rottweilers. Whilst many owners emphasise the dog's suitability as a family pet, the breed is a powerful one, they were bred to guard and can have unstable temperaments in the wrong hands. They inspire fear in many and Heather would have been aware of that.

In addition to surrounding herself with powerful symbols and freely expressing the aggressive aspects of her personality, Heather seemed to enjoy the split between her daytime and night-time personalities. There was Heather the calm professional and Heather the leather-clad biker girl.

Many therapists take the view that it is healthier for the mind to express all aspects of our personalities rather than seeking to suppress them. If we have a need to dress differently and express another side of ourselves, why not do so? Few therapists would have been alarmed by Heather's membership and active participation in a female bike group. It goes without saying that motorbike groups are made up of law-abiding enthusiasts from all walks of life yet it can't have escaped Heather's notice that there is an underlying symbolism to bikers, primarily bound up with Hell's Angels, living outside convention and even outside the law, with a heightened sense of individualism and a thirst for thrill-seeking.

There is a darker side to biker gangs that has played a part not just in the US but here in the UK. In 2007, biker Gerry Tobin was shot in the back of the head as he rode along the M40 in Warwickshire. He was travelling at ninety mph after attending a Bulldog Bash biker festival near Stratford-upon-Avon. Five members of a biker gang known as the Outlaws were found guilty of his murder. Although Heather's 'gang' had no connection to the organised crime element that exists in some segments of the biker community, Heather enjoyed the dangerous associations of biker mythology and did exploit the friendships she made through her 'Orange Pit'. Police learnt this once they searched her home and office in Crombie Avenue and found her extraordinarily detailed plans.

The stalking wasn't going well. Despite threats, cajoling, mockery and pleading, Adrian was still choosing Diane over her. She told Adrian that there was a £50,000 bounty on his head and he wasn't sure if he could dismiss this as fantasy or not. His relationship with Diane was suffering, a fact that would have delighted Heather if she had known. They did not want to separate as that would mean handing some sort of victory to a woman who was maliciously pursuing them. But few relationships could survive being under siege and Diane had been genuinely unsettled to see Heather near her children's school, camera in hand. They moved back to Radcliffe but nothing seemed to put Heather off her stride. Adrian moved out. He went to stay with a friend, and suddenly Heather seemed to have melted away.

Could it be true? Could she have simply come to her senses and given up? If she was still tracking them, it would have been obvious that Adrian and Diane were still seeing each other. But just as suddenly as Heather's deranged behaviour had begun, it seemed to have stopped.

The North of England Activity Centre is based about five miles outside York and is a popular venue for corporate days out and hen and stag parties looking for adventure, rather than just a night out drinking. It is set in thirty-four acres and offers a range of activities from archery, off-road 4x4 driving, quad biking, clay pigeon shooting and karting with full roll cages. When the centre's Philip Thompson was approached by a smartly dressed middle-aged woman with neat cropped hair, he hoped she might be booking in an activity day for a company or event. In fact, she asked about clay shooting and enquired about tuition. Phil advised that four 30-minute lessons would be a good grounding – in that way, even someone who has never handled guns can learn basic safety and handling procedures. Ms Stephenson-Snell signed up and was a model pupil.

In some ways, this shows that there was a rift between Heather's fantasy life – she had told Adrian that she was adept at handling guns and had pistols in her weapon collection – and the reality: she needed to be taught. But it does show a chilling determination to bring her revenge fantasies to life. Heather had stopped calling and contacting Adrian and Diane as she had embarked on a much more bleak endgame to her obsession with the couple. Heather was planning to murder Diane and frame her ex-boyfriend Adrian as the killer.

She planned meticulously. She worked out how to get a shotgun, how to buy the second-hand Ford and where she'd dispose of it, and she even made plans to leave both a mountain bike and a motorbike at different locations around York. The police learnt the full extent of Heather's deranged scheme once they uncovered her index cards. They make for chilling reading.

What is surprising is that at first glance this could be the work of a teenage girl, perhaps listing her favourite soap stars or DVDs. 'In Position' is the heading of one card, written in both yellow and black marker and with a bold tick-box next to it, probably to indicate that she'd completed the tasks it sets out. Under the heading, written in immature bubble writing, is 'Pink Bag', carefully coloured in with a pink felt tip. It reads:

1. Black bag (see separate card)
2. Barbie mini-skirt, skirt, tracksuit
3. Feminine but practical shoes (not white!)
4. Pink (or) Blue wig, (over *dark wig*)
5. Black PVC coat (clean off paint, fix pockets and button)
6. Thick, coloured Barbie tights
7. Pink gloves and pink scarf

This was a 45-year-old woman listing the disguises and materials she would need to carry out a murder. Pink Barbie clothing barely suitable for an eight-year-old girl was listed in a hyper-real exercise that hardly suggests blending in. A middle-aged woman riding around dressed like that even on Hallowe'en is bound to stand out. What was she thinking?

But perhaps the most disturbing detail is the note to self that the shoes, the feminine but practical shoes, should not be white. The jaunty exclamation mark a reminder that white shoes would show blood spray all too clearly. A tick follows. Heather was prepared to kill.

Another card, in red and black felt-tip markers, lists

with precise detail the route to Diane Lomax's house in Radcliffe, right down to where the costume decoy will be dropped. Heather had lost all perspective on her break-up with Adrian, she'd lost all sense of reality and rather than crawl her way back from disappointment and rejection, she had given in to her murderous desire to control the situation. Planning helped, listing all she'd need was a demonstration that she was still in command and could orchestrate events.

With the lists compiled and ticked off, decoy costumes placed in their right bags, directions to the house of her ex-lover to hand and bikes placed in friends' homes, she was ready. Heather also had some items of clothing belonging to Adrian. This is what she would wear under her white 'ghost' sheet. On one level, it was because she was staging the murder and wanted any witnesses to notice male clothing. On another deeper level, the psychology is alarming. She was dressing in her ex-lover's clothing, taking on his persona, someone she'd failed to control, to carry out what she desired – the murder of a rival.

Very few women kill and when they do it is often in a domestic setting when after years of sustained abuse, they 'snap' and lash out in an explosive moment of self-preservation. This wasn't the case with Heather, and again, it is worth examining what drove her murder plan. Since her trial, Heather has been described as 'vicious', 'psychotic' and 'wicked' but the professional in Heather would recognise these as little more than labels that may describe behaviour but not its cause. Was she suffering from a Borderline Personality Disorder and if so, why?

Abuse can trigger the development of Borderline Personality Disorder (BPD). It is a term that was first used by psychoanalyst Adolph Stern in 1938, the 'borderline' indicating behaviour that bordered on neurosis and psychosis. Suggestions have been raised that the name should be changed to 'Emotionally Unstable Personality Disorder', a more accurate reflection of the symptoms. Sufferers characterise BPD as 'black and white' thinking, erratic mood changes, reality distortion, and a tendency to display excessive behaviour such as gambling, outbursts of violence or sexual promiscuity.

Many of these characteristics are a fit with Heather's disintegrating personality and behaviour after she met Adrian. No doubt she had difficulties in the past, in her antisocial law breaking and mood swings, but her relationship with Adrian was the tipping point. Were her attempts to channel her volatility into her biker group, her drug use, her self-made drinking den and her posturing use of weaponry no longer enough? As it stood, she was forty-five years old and alone. She had been rejected and no matter her attempts to lure Adrian back, he wanted nothing more to do with her.

Her desperation may have forced a mental collapse

but she would not let her sense of self suffer. She could not. She could not tolerate the idea that she had, once again, been discarded. And so she would make Adrian the symbol of all the rejection and neglect she had suffered, the object of her fury. He would pay.

The sexual element of the rejection cannot be overlooked. The threats she made against Diane were explicitly sexual, such as stating she would cut off her breasts. Symbolically, she was threatening to remove Diane's sexual potency, something she feared was waning in herself. She seduced Adrian on the night of his return once she'd arrived back from New York. No doubt she felt this was all she needed to do to guarantee his return to her domain. When that failed, the stakes were raised. At the murder trial that followed, Heather's defence team alleged that she had been provoked after Adrian had raped her. Adrian's answer is revealing. He said: 'No, I did not rape her. If anything, it was more the other way round.'

Later, he spoke about feeling like a 'guinea pig' during their brief relationship. Heather talked to him about his troubled past, took notes and would have had no doubt that he was emotionally vulnerable. Perfect, in fact, for her to manipulate as she chose. But something went wrong and this 'weak' man had the strength to walk away and see Heather for what she was; an ageing fraud.

All this scrolled through Heather's fractured mind as she climbed into the Ford Escort and turned the key in the ignition. She pulled out of her driveway, the start of a seventy-three-mile journey that she calculated would take her one hour and twenty-five minutes. At her side was the pink bag, the sheet, Scream mask, shotgun and bike helmet. It was after eleven when she left; a good time to drive as the roads were so quiet.

Heather pulled up into Holland Street at around twelve thirty a.m. This was the culmination of eighteen months of anger. Someone was going to pay.

Adrian was not staying with Diane and her children that evening. He was elsewhere as the scene contrived in his name unfolded. But Bob Wilkie was with his fiancée and was woken up by the hammering next door. Nursing the gun with one arm, Heather banged on Diane's door. What was taking her so long? Even now, this last night, she was not doing as Heather wanted. She was probably hiding behind the door having sneaked a look out of the window and guessing that whoever it was thundering at the door, she should not open it.

Bob had had enough. Opening the door of Debbie's house, he stepped straight onto the pavement, as there was no front garden or gate, so in a moment he was at Heather's side. She did not expect that. Hearing Bob's voice, hearing him take charge of the situation, Diane felt confident to open the door. The figure was turned away, arguing with Bob. He pulled at the mask and that was it. One moment. In one moment, Bob had taken control and torn through Heather's carefully laid plans, all her pretence and threats. She was a little woman standing in men's clothes, looking foolish. It didn't matter who the target was any more, someone had to pay for the madness; anyone but Heather.

It was over. She stood with another man's blood running off her sheet, the mask discarded, her face battered from losing grip as the gun recoiled. She could not even control that.

Women were screaming as she walked away. She attempted her escape and, in her effort to manipulate appearances, to not be seen to be fleeing the scene, she slowed to a crawl along the M62.

The case came to trial in September 2004. By then, Adrian and Diane's relationship had broken down, neither could live with the impact of Heather's harassment, and Diane in particular struggled with the memory of her neighbour Bob Wilkie lying dead from his chest wound. Bob's fiancée and brother paid tribute to a wonderful, kind, loving partner, brother and loyal friend to many.

The contrast of statements made about Heather could not have been more dramatic. The trial judge, Mr Justice Wakerley, described her murder plans and her lies to the court as 'breathtaking'. He also highlighted that she showed 'no hint of remorse' and sentenced her to a minimum of twenty-two years for the murder of Bob Wilkie and the attempted murder of Diane Lomax.

The police were no less damning. Detective Superintendent Simon Barraclough characterised her as 'a jealous woman who went out on Hallowe'en intent on causing pain and suffering'. He also said that she 'told a series of continued and sustained lies while she was in police custody and during the course of her trial'. And just in case anyone imagined that this was a common case of a spurned lover taking bloody revenge, he added that Heather was 'one of the most peculiar individuals I have ever had to deal with'.

Indeed she was, but by then Heather was beyond caring. She had left her persona as a respectable mother and working professional for good. It was a persona that she had used but discarded, she imagined, in the name of love, but what she did bore no resemblance to love except in her fractured mind. Her crisis and what caused it would now haunt her and the families of Bob Wilkie, Diane Lomax and Adrian Sinclair for ever.

CHAPTER THREE

Edith McAlinden
House of Blood

In violence we forget who we are
Mary McCarthy

'Give me some money, Pops, I need to get my boy here.'

When Ian Mitchell heard these words, he had little idea that a bad evening was about to detonate into an night of frenzied violence. A night that would leave three men dead in one small flat. A night that would only end when a woman was found by police officers cradling a dead man. She was sitting, rocking a man's body in her arms, shouting: 'Wake up, wake up!' It was the only sound in the flat. All the officers gathered in the front room were silent, unable to take in all they could see. Later, a senior detective with thirty years' service could only describe it as the most chilling murder scene he'd ever visited.

It all unfolded in the early hours of 17 October 2004. As the hours ticked by into Sunday morning, a call was put through to the duty detective, Detective Superintendent Willie Johnston. He was told that a woman was in custody after she was discovered in a flat in Dixon Road, in the Crosshill area of Glasgow. She told the police that a fight had broken out between three men: her boyfriend and two men who lived at the flat, 67-year-old Ian Mitchell and 71-year-old Tony Coyle. The boyfriend was identified as 42-year-old David Gillespie and at first what seemed to link the three men was that they were all heavy drinkers. Something must have happened between them, probably a spark of a disagreement that erupted into alcohol-fuelled violence.

Willie Johnston was no stranger to the worst excesses of violence and disorder in his patch of what is frequently described as a troubled city. No city is without its problems and no city can be characterised by a simple headline or two. It rankles with all those who work and live in Glasgow to hear it routinely described as the 'murder capital of Western Europe'. Those working to promote the city point out that in an American business survey in 2008, Glasgow was judged the best city in the UK for safety and quality of life. The survey is used by businesses assessing risk for employees who travel around the world and, indeed, Glasgow's commercial districts and affluent suburbs are safe. But Ian Davidson, Labour MP for Glasgow South West, noted the apparent contradiction and said: 'Glasgow is a safe city for the prosperous.'

Glasgow has its troubled areas. Areas that suffer from low employment, high drug and alcohol dependency, recreational violence and rising rates of mental health problems. There is no quick fix. And the impact on those who live in disadvantaged areas can be catastrophic.

The state of housing is frequently raised by community campaigners hoping to see changes in Crosshill and Govanhill. Complaints of persistent fly-tipping that is not stopped or cleared up; mattresses dumped into alleyways, and cellars in tenement flats piled high with fetid items cast off by people who drift in and out of low-rent accommodation. Complaining of litter and poor housing stock may seem minor but for the vast majority of people living in the area it is the first sign that a neighbourhood is in decline. It shows that residents feel little pride in where they live and what follows is sure to be a disregard for others.

It didn't happen overnight. Crosshill, south of the River Clyde, was once farmland and only became residential after the 1850s with the rapid growth of Glasgow's middle class. This was an affluent suburb with fewer than three thousand residents until the expansion of the railway in the 1880s. The boom in shipbuilding and engineering saw Glasgow's population grow at an unparalleled rate and by the start of the twentieth century it was outranked by only London, Paris and Berlin.

To accommodate the rise in numbers, red sandstone tenement buildings were built to house workers. They had high ceilings, large rooms and the kind of period features sought out by today's middle class, but Glasgow's industrial base was vulnerable to recession. Throughout the twentieth century the city continued to decline; unable to innovate and keep pace with industrial advances being made across the globe, thousands of jobs were lost and the once proud tenements gradually became bywords for unemployment and poor housing. Gradually, the three-storey houses were divided up into smaller and smaller units that were populated by an emerging underclass, where work was scarce and welfare the norm.

Glasgow has tried to diversify its economic base over the last thirty years, pushing into financial services and creating initiatives to regenerate inner cities, the high rises and tenements. There has been a resurgent middle class and many of the city's Victorian villas have been re-gentrified. But as one youth community worker from an area yet to benefit from the economic rebirth cautioned: 'I got to see for myself what can happen to an area when it's left to rot over a generation.'

Dependence on drink and drugs has spiralled over

the decades. Almost half of the murders police in Strath-clyde deal with have been committed under the influ-ence of drink and drugs. One generation out of work and living on state handouts passes its despair to the next and crime and violence are the ever-present by-products of disintegrating communities. The police called to the flat on Dixon Avenue on 17 October 2004 were no strangers to the worst excesses that their patch could throw up. Only six months earlier, they'd dealt with a tenement fire that tore through a building in Allison Street, just a few minutes away, that had been set deliberately by 24-year-old Samuel Petto.

Petto had been drinking heavily and had started a row with 30-year-old Arthur Rawlinson. Petto had lost some money and was convinced that Rawlinson, a father of five, had hidden it. It led to the two men argu-ing in the street. Rawlinson had recently been released from prison and was staying in one of the tenements – Petto followed him into the flat and the fight esca-lated. It ended once Petto had stabbed Rawlinson repeatedly. Rather than call for help, Petto recruited two friends and they set fire to the ground floor by dous-ing it with petrol. It caused an explosion, ripping glass from window panes and sending up a fireball and black smoke that would trap many in the building.

Myra Donachie was one of the residents unable to escape. The 52-year-old lived above Rawlinson and she would be the second fatality of the evening. Ten others were hurt before firefighters could control the blaze. Mrs Donachie's daughter Yvonne was also badly hurt. Her son, Stephen, said: 'It's been a tragic loss for our family. No one could have said a bad word about my mother or my sister. It was like someone had hit me with a baseball bat when they said, "You haven't got a ma any more".'

Petto was arrested three days after the fire. He was spotted on CCTV one hour before the blast, buying three petrol containers. The case came to trial in October and on the fourth, Petto pleaded guilty pleaded guilty to the culpable homicide of Arthur Rawlinson and Myra Donachie and was jailed for eighteen years.

Myra Donachie was an innocent casualty of Crosshill's violent undercurrent. Police were sure that she would not be the last and, sure enough, less than two weeks had passed when a call came from a tenement flat on Dixon Road. The caller said that a woman had banged on his door asking for help. She'd called around to see her boyfriend who was visiting a mutual friend. There'd been a fight.

It was a story that, at first, was accepted at face value. The woman, a 36-year-old called Edith McAlinden, was found nursing 42-year-old David Gillespie, her boyfriend. The top-floor flat belonged not to him but to a retired joiner called Ian Mitchell. He was sixty-seven years old and was divorced. For the last ten years, he'd rented out his spare room to retired labourer Tony Coyle, originally from Donegal in Ireland but resident of Glasgow for most of his adult life. Both men were seasoned drinkers but neither had a reputation as troublemakers and both were well-liked.

Less was known about David Gillespie. His association with Mitchell and Coyle seemed a recent arrangement. It was Edith who'd found the three men. It looked as if Gillespie had been stabbed in the leg and an almighty fight had followed. Who could tell who set about whom? The other two men were older but they'd laboured around the building trade for all of their working lives and could handle themselves. Edith was distraught about David. He would not wake up. The call was made, the emergency services were on their way.

The first police officers at the scene struggled for words. They were going to need a lot more help. No one was moving but Edith. Three men lay dead in one small sitting room. This was no ordinary scene. This wasn't a stumble or push that had led to a fatal head injury. This wasn't punches thrown and unintentional damage caused. This was utter carnage. No surface was left untouched. Every wall bloodstained, every object in the room upended, furniture smashed, blood covered the floor and walls, blood spray could even be seen on the ceiling.

Then there were the weapons. A baseball bat, knives,

a golf club, a hammer, wooden slats, bottles, a belt, an axe and an electric drill. And amongst the empty bottles and wrecked furniture, sitting in the middle of the room, was an electric kettle.

The culmination of gruesome details, the sight of three battered men, the screaming woman, the walls smeared with blood and body tissue, were simply too much to take in. Edith would not calm down, would not stop screaming. The paramedics needed to attend to the man she was gripping and holding close to her and the measured requests the police made to her to let him go were not making any headway.

Edith would not stop rocking and shouting for Gillespie to wake up. One officer tried to pick her up off the sofa and she lashed out savagely. Her attention had flipped from the man she was holding to the police officer and she began screaming incoherently. Edith had to have her arms pinned back and when the threat of arrest did not cut through her rage, she found herself handcuffed. It seemed incomprehensible. The officers had attended the bereaved before, even those with a history of violence, but this was something else. Edith McAlinden was awash with hatred for everyone who stood in the small and soiled flat.

She was arrested for a breach of the peace and once in custody it was soon clear that this was not the first brush Edith had had with the police. She was an inveterate offender and had a string of arrests from affray to theft and assault. She was effectively homeless, and not just because she had recently been released after serving nine months of a prison sentence. Edith had drifted in and out of hostels and temporary accommodation for some years.

Her attitude when questioned showed all the hardened disregard that develops in many who have been shunted around the fringes of society since childhood. A noxious mix of familiarity and contempt. She would not be intimidated by arrest and questioning, it was all too routine. She looked at those sitting opposite her with barely contained disdain.

Edith's story mirrored the one she'd offered up to Ian Mitchell's neighbour, James Sweeney. He was struggling to process all he'd seen once he'd agreed to follow Edith back to the flat. 'Something's gone wrong, Jim,' she told him, and it surely had. He staggered from the flat and called the police.

Edith made her statement: She knew Ian, she called him Pops, he was pretty good to her and would let her crash at his flat and enjoy a drinking session for a few hours. She had not been out of jail long – she'd been in for nine months and was staying in hostels until she got back on her feet. David Gillespie was her boyfriend at the moment; he was separated from his partner and kids and he and Edith got along fine.

She'd taken David up to Pops's flat, he'd been there maybe two or three times before. The three of them had a few drinks. Tony the lodger wasn't there but must have come back at some point. Edith didn't know because she'd left after a couple of hours. She was going to see if she could get a few more drinks in but when she'd got back, she realised some sort of fight must have broken out. No idea over what. Perhaps David didn't like the way Pops was talking about Edith. It must have been an almighty fight, true enough, and it looked like Tony the lodger joined in, maybe to split them up, but something went wrong. It's hard to know. She just found them that way and ran to get Jim Sweeney.

By the time Edith's statement was being processed, all the agencies involved in every serious crime investigation were going through the motions. The scene was sealed, the bodies had been removed to pathology for post-mortem, photographers were producing 360-degree room-by-room images, forensics took samples and began an assessment of the blood spray patterns and police officers were making door-to-door enquiries and taking statements. There was still a lot to learn about the three men and Edith McAlinden.

The Scottish legal system differs from that of England and Wales. In Scotland, the police produce an initial report for a Procurator Fiscal who then assesses whether there is sufficient evidence for the case to be prosecuted. On a practical level, the Procurator Fiscal has also to act as investigator, reviewing forensic evidence and interviewing witnesses. In this case, the Procurator

Fiscal asked to visit the scene, a routine request. She found it impossible to stay. No matter the number of years served, everyone involved in the case was shocked by the flat that was soon dubbed the 'House of Blood' by local press.

And this was before the press had any inkling of the pathology reports. The police were told that it took hours to list the injuries the men had sustained. 'Blunt force trauma' was listed, indicating that the men had been beaten with objects and that they had been beaten without remorse. What was more, there was evidence that the men had had boiling water poured onto them. The detectives recalled the strange sight of the electric kettle sitting in the middle of the front room and realised why it was there.

The pathologist also noted that David Gillespie had received two savage knife blows to his legs, one of which severed a femoral artery. He had consumed a great deal of alcohol and, piecing together other evidence available from the scene, it seemed that Gillespie had simply stayed on the sofa and bled to death.

The scenario Edith had painted was falling apart. If Gillespie had remained on the sofa, what had happened to the two other men? It seemed that Gillespie did not show signs of having attacked either Mitchell or Coyle. So who did? At first it was possible to imagine that a fight had broken out but as details emerged, too many features were not accounted for, such as the blood-soaked sofa that Gillespie appeared not to have moved from, and who had been responsible for pouring boiling water over Mitchell and Coyle.

The one person in custody, Edith McAlinden, yielded nothing under questioning. She stuck resolutely to her version of events. Yet officers were sure that she could not have committed the triple murder alone; it was an event of ferocious and single-minded violence but it seemed doubtful that one women could have murdered three men – there must have been others involved. They examined Edith's life and it didn't take long before it became clear who she would turn to. She had a son.

Edith was little more than a child herself when she gave birth to her son, John. Perhaps she hoped that John would fill her life with all the love that she'd never experienced once he was born. There is little evidence that John's father played a part in his upbringing. It is believed that Edith had tried to make a life for herself on the streets since she was ten. A neglected and troubled child, she took to drinking at a young age and struggled to provide for John. She made money where she could; there were rumours that she turned tricks if she had to – robbing drunk men of what they had in their pockets, stealing stuff – and that she could hold her own. People learnt not to cross her, she'd a temper if pushed and could give as good as she got.

As John reached his teens, many people noted that they looked so alike, they could even be mistaken for brother and sister, both fair-haired and blue-eyed. Despite a chaotic childhood, John adored his ma. John would doing anything for her. Anything at all.

When she'd come out of prison that last time, he was there for her, he and his best pal Jamie Gray – they were close enough for John to call him his brother – and they all went out on a session. John and Jamie had been friends for a long while, they'd been in trouble a few times with the law but not for anything major, just the usual accusations of petty thefts and the odd fight or two. He could take care of himself, just like his ma.

To the outside observer, what John shared with his mother was a destructive cycle of offending and few skills to help break it. Edith had served her sentence for serious assault and at the time of her release, John was staying in a homeless hostel in the city, near St Enoch's Square. Although well-meaning, the hostels are rarely an ideal environment for offenders and addicts. Most know they are housed there as an emergency measure, supposedly for eight to twelve weeks, but many stay for months until drifting on to the next emergency shelter.

The intensive support and guidance required to help hostel residents change their lives for the better is simply not available. Occasionally, initiatives and projects will be on hand for some but funding is erratic. At the heart of the issue is addressing behaviour that is entrenched. Each individual will have different and complex sets of needs, amassed over years, from a damaged and excluded childhood, to adulthood where offending and abuse is the norm. Rarely will it be altered after three weeks of art therapy alone.

Hostels prevent people from sleeping on the streets but the lack of permanency often feeds a destructive cycle. And it is clear that they are not wanted. Residents in the areas surrounding hostels wish they were elsewhere, and not without reason. Market-stall holders near the hostel that housed John McAlinden put together crime figures from a single year. There were 314 drug possession cases, 29 robberies, 96 thefts, 89 assaults, 268 breaches of the peace, 46 cases of police assault and resisting arrest and one attempted murder. They laid this wholly at the door of the hostel's transient residents; whether that was fair was by the by.

Attitudes are set on both sides of the divide and as one café owner at the market said: 'There are times when we need to chase junkies away from our stalls and some of them can get violent – but why should we be policing the area?'

Out of this sense of exclusion and hostility came Edith and John McAlinden.

Edith had been drinking but she needed more. She'd called in on Pops, someone she'd used before. The dynamic was always the same for Edith. She'd reel men in, let them think that they were on to a good thing with her, then she'd have sex with them if she needed to keep the flow of cash and have a place to stay – it meant little to her and it meant that they were stupid enough to imagine that they were the ones pulling the strings. Before too long, it was clear that Edith called the shots. If they made a fuss, she'd no problem expressing her needs violently.

It worked out well enough for Pops at first. Here was a woman, not bad looking either, willing to entertain him as long as the drink and the odd cash handout kept coming. Old Tony Coyle wasn't fooled by her and saw her as trouble but Tony had never offended anyone in his life. He'd lived happily as a lodger with Ian for ten years and now that he'd retired, only six months previously, he didn't want that to change. He kept his mouth shut and himself out of the way when Edith came to call, it was easier that way.

When Edith knocked on his door with David Gillespie, Ian Mitchell knew that he had little choice but to let them in. He hoped for no trouble. Tony was out at a local pub and Ian resigned himself to the fact that his visitors were here to stay until the drink ran out. It started well enough – Edith could be good fun when she wanted to, cracking jokes and full of smiles. But drink is unpredictable. It can propel some into feeling jovial but it can take nothing for the mood to darken, a remark made and the wrong thing inferred from it. It was never intended, but offence is caused. Even the request for calm becomes an affront, an apology goes unregistered.

Something in the atmosphere of the flat must have changed that night. Perhaps a flippant remark went wide of the mark. Edith was quick to anger and perhaps Gillespie laughed, trying to diffuse the situation but it badly misfired. Edith would not take disrespect from anyone. She walked into Mitchell's kitchen, leaving Gillespie on the sofa. When she came back into the room, she had a knife in her hand. Gillespie would have seen little, until it was too late. Edith stabbed him in each leg.

The couple had been drinking all day. Gillespie did not move. Shock mixed with fear: if he stood up, she might have continued her attack; he would have quickly become light-headed from the amount of alcohol swimming in his system and from the rapid blood loss from his severed femoral artery. Blood drained into the sofa, he would have had no idea that the rate was so rapid, but then neither did his drinking companions.

Ian Mitchell would have seen it all. He would have seen Edith snap and watched her come back into the front room, it is unlikely that he had time to react as she used the knife to slice into the younger man's legs. He would have feared that Edith's attention would switch to him. Mitchell may well have tried to buy time, hoping that Edith would have given in to inebriation. That would have been his best hope of getting out and calling for help. Edith sat down next to Gillespie and began chatting again.

But what Mitchell could not have known was that Edith's mind churned even faster than his. She saw what she had done. She was at risk of going back to prison again. What could she do about Pops? Gillespie slumped onto the arm of the sofa, his legs still extended to the floor. There were dark pools on both legs of his jeans. No, she could not trust Pops to keep his mouth shut. He had never been in trouble with the police; Edith may well have guessed that Mitchell would have given it all up with the first set of questions.

'Give me some money, Pops, I need to get my boy here,' Edith asked with a smile. Sure enough, Mitchell reached for his wallet, hoping perhaps that she was making ready to leave, seeking out the next drink. Edith stood up, stepped out of the room, and made a phone call. But it wasn't to the emergency services, things had gone too far for that. She called John and said: 'Get over here, I need you to do something for me.'

It took the best part of forty minutes before the taxi arrived with the two teenagers, and Edith kept Mitchell hemmed into the flat, probably with a mix of menace and camaraderie. She took the money from Mitchell to pay for the taxi. This was the last chance for Mitchell but he could never second-guess what Edith had said in her phone call, he had no idea that she filled her boy's ear with a tale of attempted rape and the instruction that he and Jamie should come armed for retribution, no idea at all.

The boys were fired up. They had brought what they needed to sort out the old man. The attack was ferocious. With Edith directing, they set about the 67-year-old with an array of weapons. He fought hard for his life. They bludgeoned him with a baseball bat, with a clump of wood John had found, and with their feet. Mitchell tried to avoid the blows, crawling towards the door, his arms registering massive damage as he attempted to protect himself. His face ballooned beyond recognition and he began to choke on blood blocking his airways. Then Edith heard footsteps along the hallway. They stopped.

It was Tony Coyle. He opted for an earlier night than usual. He was ready for his bed. Once he entered the flat, it was too late. If he'd seen something, if he'd heard his friend Ian call out, it might have been different. He could have slammed the door and run. But that wasn't to be. The flat was quiet but there was a strange and muffled noise of something in pain and he walked into hell. The front door was blocked by one of the attackers, they could not let him go. He ran, instead, to his room, and locked the door.

What happened next staggered the police. Tony's room had a decent lock on it and the door could not be broken down despite their attempts to kick it through. But Tony had no mobile phone, he could not call the police, he was trapped. Edith knew she and the boys were trapped too. She had to get the old man out of the room. They had tried force but it didn't work. They got Mitchell's electric drill and tried to remove the hinges but that failed too. Edith had another weapon and she brought it in to play. She removed the boys from the door and started talking.

She talked to Tony through the door. She could hear him praying. She took her time and said there'd been a terrible mistake, that she'd pulled the boys off and calmed the whole situation down. She was sorry things got out of hand and she was ready to leave. If he were to come out and see if he could help her, see how best to help his friend Ian, she promised that no harm would come to him. She gave her word. She sobbed and said she was so worried about Ian and David. She said the boys had run off now and she didn't want to be left alone not knowing how to help Ian. He could die.

Tony Coyle opened his door and walked out. Edith gave the signal and the boys fell savagely on the 71-year-old. He pleaded and he prayed once more but they had no mercy in their souls. As he crawled along the passageway, a golf club was used to smash his skull repeatedly. Police would later film the club where it lay with bloodstained tufts of hair stuck to it, next to a knife with flesh stuck to the handle and blade.

Like his friend, Tony Coyle fought. He'd known a life of physical hardship and labour but his strength would not prove enough. The boy who'd left a simple farm in Donegal years ago, who'd worked every day of his life, would breathe his last in a blood-filled flat on Dixon Avenue. His brothers and sisters would never come to terms with the attack. Nobody had a bad word to say about Tony. How could his life be brought to such a pitiless end?

It's doubtful that even Edith knew. She had orchestrated the attack and now that it was ended, she was unsure of herself once more. She was sobering up and that didn't help. She had to know that the men, the witnesses to her crimes, were really dead. Were they faking it? Another trick, someone else who thought they'd get the better of her. They held a cushion over Coyle's face and stood on it. Then Edith told John to put the kettle on.

The boys watched as she poured the boiling water on Mitchell and Coyle. No movement. Time to think 'what next?'

She told the two boys that they should leave; they needed to be well clear of what happened and she'd sort out the rest. With the boys gone, Edith prepared her story and waited until she was ready to walk down to Jim's flat. She'd tell him that there must have been a fight.

Sitting in the police interview suite over a number of sessions, Edith's story didn't change. But outside, progress was being made. There were sightings of two young men on Dixon Avenue, making their way from a cab and to the tenement block. There was some CCTV evidence of their movements. Then there was a state-ment given by one of the other men that shared the hostel with John McAlinden. John had returned to St Enoch's Square and told him: 'Stabbed a guy in the legs, man. There was blood everywhere. It was a fella tried to rape my ma. So I had to teach him a lesson, eh.'

He had no doubt that John was telling the truth, or at least part of it, and knew that something was very wrong. He cooperated with the police who had by this time established that the one relative Edith was in contact with was her son John.

Yet even then the case wasn't without its twists. When John and his associate, Jamie Gray, were brought in for questioning, senior detectives doubted they could be involved in such an horrific slaying. Both were ques-tioned and both gave a plausible explanation of their movements that evening. They had been on Dixon Avenue, and had even been to the flat to see Edith during one of her previous visits, but had no idea of what had happened there later that evening.

What was difficult to grasp was the idea that two sixteen-year-old boys, guilty of only minor offences, could then arm themselves and take part in a sustained and frenzied attack of this nature. They had taken cloth-ing from the boys but there was some uncertainty that the forensic lab would be able to substantiate the suspi-cion that they had been involved that night.

Yet the examination of their clothing would prove

damning. The clothes had been cleaned but it wasn't enough to disguise what had occurred. There was blood spray from the victims, particularly concentrated around the bottom of their jeans and on their footwear. Put together with the aerial patterns that had been examined, it was clear that they had both participated in the attack and had kicked and stamped on the men repeatedly.

With the leverage of physical evidence placing the boys in the flat that evening, they were both turned. Even then, there was no remorse, the statements they gave were minimal and neither could give any insight into why the killings had been so brutal.

John missed his ma. In the eyes of one senior detective, Edith would not have hesitated in turning John over if it would help her stay outside prison but her son was blind to that. As it stood, all three were charged with the triple murder and waited for their trial date.

A triple murder is rare and it is also difficult to prosecute as it is not easy to prove who was responsible for which death. Edith remained hostile but resigned as the wheels of justice slowly turned. She seemed bored by the whole process.

The trial began seven months later in May 2005 at Glasgow's High Court. The prosecution began their arguments and Isher Singh Dass, a bus driver who lived in the flat below Ian Mitchell's, told that court how his ceiling shook and that he heard a 'noise like thunder' before the three men were found dead. The defendants looked unperturbed. When the police video was shown of the carnage inside the flat, all three were seen to laugh. The ashen-faced jury were enough to convince the defence team that their clients should consider changing their plea.

They duly did. They entered a separate plea of guilty to one murder each. Edith McAlinden pleaded guilty to the murder of David Gillespie, her son to the murder of Ian Mitchell and Jamie Gray to killing Tony Coyle. The sentencing that followed a month later appalled the families of the victims. Although all were given life sentences, the teenage boys were advised that their minimum tariff would be twelve years and Edith McAlinden would serve a minimum of thirteen years.

Violet Cahill was David Gillespie's partner for twenty years, until they went their separate ways and he met Edith. He was the father of her children and she told reporters that they still cry at night over the loss of their father. Although separated, David and Violet were on good terms and David had even saved up to buy her a freezer when Violet's had broken down. She echoed the sentiment of many when she said of the jail terms: 'I am just disgusted, yet they go down the stairs laughing as if the whole thing is a big joke. There are animals on the street better than these people. They are scum.'

Ms Cahill had to watch them laugh when the images were shown in court. They were so removed from their actions, from their terrifying lack of humanity that they could only find it funny. Just how damaged these three individuals were before the night they chose murder is open to speculation. The police are sure that Edith choreographed the whole evening. One senior detective described Edith as a 'black widow', someone who saw lying, theft, violence and deception as a way of life. Pops and David were there to be ripped off, and then they simply got in the way, as did Tony Coyle.

Edith still has no idea of the evil she unleashed that night, no idea how much she devastated the families of her victims. She seems to have adapted to prison life well and her letters to John have been leaked to the press. 'Keep the grin above the chin!' she wrote in a girlish script. She also adds that they are both part of the 'Anti-screw crew 110%', and decorates her letters and parcels to him with smiley faces and slogans.

Perhaps she does not have the capacity for remorse. Edith was a profoundly damaged human being long before that Saturday 16 October. Life in an abusive home and life on the streets had hollowed out any chance she had to be a caring and functioning woman. She may believe that she loved her son but she never had the emotional resources to help him become a healthy human being. Once she was in trouble, she called him and destroyed his life as surely as she destroyed everything else she touched that night.

John was her one hope to be a better person, to create a life better than she ever knew but she failed at this as she had with everything else. All ended in rage. A rage so catastrophic that she could forget everything for that brief time. She wasn't an alcoholic failure, a street casualty with no home and no future. For that brief hour of carnage, she was in control and all there would feel her rage. Then it ended. She is left only with horror.

CHAPTER FOUR

Jacqui and Kelly Noble
Like Mother, Like Daughter

A bad ending follows a bad beginning
Euripides

A hot June day in Laytown isn't to be wasted. The Irish coastal town boasts some of the best beaches in Ireland but, as you're as likely to encounter rain in June as you are sunshine, on this fine day a lot of people made the effort to travel to the seaside resort from the surrounding villages. Amongst them was nineteen-year-old mother of two Emma McLoughlin who'd hopped on the bus at Drogheda. She planned an afternoon of fun. She was in a great mood. It did not seem possible that within hours she would her lose her life at the hands of another young mother.

Emma had spent the afternoon drinking with her

sister and a friend. They'd larked around and as the hours passed, had consumed a fair but not excessive amount of alcohol, including vodka, cider and lager, so Emma decided to call into a nearby supermarket to buy some snacks as she wasn't ready for the day to end. Turning the corner of one of the aisles, she spotted Kelly Noble. Seeing the young woman changed her mood entirely.

All the pent-up antagonism she harboured from an old argument they'd had rose up in her again. The cause of the row went back some three years but standing in the aisle of the supermarket it hit her as if new. Emma was going to get answers from the woman and she was going to get them now. Kelly had her back to her and was pushing a buggy as Emma marched up behind her.

Emma got her way. The row started up again but she would never have guessed that it would end as it did. Within ten minutes, Emma would receive a single stab wound to the chest, it would pierce her heart and she would die at the roadside.

What was extraordinary about the case was that Kelly Noble didn't have a knife as she wheeled her young son into Pat's supermarket but once she saw Emma and felt the row would escalate, she simply called a friend and asked her to bring one. This friend, Niamh Cullen, slotted a kitchen knife into a school bag and walked the few hundred yards from her home to deliver it to Kelly. She had to walk to the store with Kelly's other young child and so, hand in hand, with a weapon in a satchel, Niamh imagined she was helping to protect her friend. She never imagined that she was helping her to end the life of another young mother.

As news leaked out about the murder, local residents were outraged. How could such a brutal and senseless killing have taken place? Yet as the facts emerged, shock gave way to sorrowful resignation. There was a sad inevitability, a recognition that when Emma met Kelly that night, it was only ever going to end one way.

Kelly Noble was arrested for murder. She was twenty years old and was no stranger to violence. She knew Emma, they had a number of run-ins over the years and the night of 2 June 2006 was merely the last. Staff at the supermarket gave the police a full account of all they saw as neither Kelly nor Emma hid their antagonism – this was a very open hostility between the two. Yet scratch beneath the surface of their feud and they had so much in common: both had two children they adored, both were trying to make a place in the world for themselves and both struggled to contain their demons.

It is understandable that Emma McLoughlin's family want to emphasise only the positive aspects of their daughter's life. She was loved and is desperately missed. Thomas McLoughlin said that the loss of his daughter had left a 'huge hole' in his heart and that everyone who knew Emma was traumatised by her murder. Those who have suffered most are the ones who were too young to understand what happened: Emma's children, five-year-old Holly and two-year-old Jack. The little ones had to be placed in foster care as Emma's mother became too ill to care for them full-time. It is a tragic outcome but it is not the full picture.

Emma McLoughlin was known to the Garda (the Irish police). She had been dealt with through the juvenile liaison scheme and a diagnosis of ADHD was put forward to explain her occasional loss of temper. At the trial, Emma's track record would be described as less than enviable but it was a family member who provided the most disturbing evidence of how catastrophic her anger could be.

Shona McLoughlin, a year younger than her sister Emma, had been a drinking companion on the day of her death. She would later deny that Emma was violent yet in court admitted that she had made a previous statement to gardaí describing how her sister had broken her jaw and kicked her during a disagreement over a mobile phone. Emma had accused Shona of stealing her phone. Sensing her sister's rising anger, Shona hid the phone up her sleeve just before Emma lashed out. From the outside, this was no minor altercation. Shona was left with a swelling to her brain and was briefly hospitalised. Yet soon after her release from hospital, Shona patched things up with Emma and she did not wish to press charges.

Shona's decision to carry on as if nothing had happened may puzzle some but perhaps not those who have lived with children or siblings with ADHD. In many ways it is a misunderstood condition as diagnosis is based on behavioural characteristics rather than an easily identifiable neurological disease. It has been dismissed by some as a modern label for naughty children – children that are disruptive, inattentive and aggressive and who need to learn some self-control. In fact, many scientific papers have mapped the condition, it is real and the behavioural problems displayed by those with ADHD may be a result of differences in the frontal lobes, the area of the brain that controls impulses.

Typically, children with ADHD are disruptive in school, can be aggressive, immature and clumsy. As they reach adolescence, the inability to process risk can lead to self-harm, accidents, substance misuse and delinquency. Yet family members also report that once the moment of rage has passed, the ADHD child or adolescent can be bright, loving, exuberant and good company. For siblings, ADHD is difficult but most learn to adapt and accept that their loving, loyal and fun brother or sister has outbursts of aggression and recklessness.

Despite a sometimes troubled relationship, losing Emma devastated Shona and she felt honour-bound to defend her memory. No matter how bad Emma's temper could be, nothing justified Kelly's brutal attack. Asked again about her sister's temperament Shona said: 'I don't really want to talk about it. It is nothing got to do with you.'

To an outsider, Emma was a troublemaker but for those who knew her best, trouble was never sought, it was just something Emma would stumble into without thinking through how she might be jeopardising her safety or that of others. Her family had always be on hand to help her deal with the consequences, Emma was loved and perhaps it was something that Kelly noticed. They looked out for one another. No matter the hardship or the disagreements, they put each other first. This stood in sharp contrast to Kelly's early life.

By the time Kelly Noble was born, the odds against her ever enjoying a normal family life were minimal. Both her parents were heroin addicts. Jacqui Noble and Derek Benson could have taken the news that they were to become parents as an opportunity to break from their addiction and start afresh, but it wasn't to be.

The two, barely out of their teens, were already locked into a destructive and abusive relationship that would only end fourteen years later, when one of them was found hacked to death. It would take a further four years before the full facts of that murder were heard in court.

Kelly was Jacqui's only child. Like many children born

to addicts, she learnt early in life that she came second in her parents' attentions, the need to feed their drug habit always came first. Assessing whether to keep babies in the care of drug-addicted parents has long posed a dilemma for social services. Mothers want to turn over a new leaf and often romanticise what it will mean to have a baby that will 'love them unconditionally', something often missing from their own upbringing.

The reality of mothering a newborn frequently proves too stressful for recovering addicts and the temptation to return to an insulating addiction proves too strong. As the mother struggles to cope with the 'failure' to break her habit and the demands of motherhood, the baby can become an object of blame and neglect.

Those who work in social services do their best, through monitoring, assessment and support but horror stories hit the news headlines year in year out. Reports such as nine-month-old Perrin Barlow who was found dead in his mother's flat in Plymouth. Stephanie Horrocks's neglect allowed her son to die of a simple chest infection brought on by malnutrition and dehydration. In the same year, 2007, fourteen-month-old Rio Ross was found dead clutching a Winnie the Pooh toy after a fatal overdose of heroin, cocaine and methadone. His mother, Sabrina Ross, admitted manslaughter and had her second son placed in care.

The name of one mother from Dublin could not be released even as her case was brought to court. Her son was found on a bed in a sodden nappy with blood around his nose and mouth, surrounded by empty beer cans and that unmistakable sign of heroin use – a burnt spoon. His mother pleaded guilty to wilfully neglecting the child at Dublin Circuit Criminal Court in December 2005 but could not be named to protect the identity of her other six children.

Even if children of addicts survive physically, the emotional impact of their early years is only now being fully understood. The impact of neglect on the mind of a developing child has become scientifically measurable. Magnetic resonance imaging (MRI) gathered over the last decade suggests that a child's brain development is directly affected by the way they are cared for.

It is something that primary school teachers have spoken about for years. They take in children at four and five years and can tell, from day one, those that are already damaged. The child that can't concentrate, the child with erratic and violent mood swings, the child that can't communicate and is easily distressed. Off the record, teachers speak of the heartache of trying to 'rewire' a child from a dysfunctional and chaotic household. Through MRI, anecdotal reference to how a child is 'wired' has turned out to be rooted in an electrochemical fact.

We all develop a 'baseline', an electrochemical mix that is our 'normal' state of mind and a point that we return to after being distressed or excitable. Children who have been maltreated or neglected register reduced function in key areas of the brain, such as the hippocampus, an area used to store and retrieve emotional memory. All children have to be taught how to deal with stressful situations, and those who fare best are those who have been taught through consistent and caring parenting. Those who are neglected struggle to regulate how they feel and cope, not just as children but as they mature. The stakes get higher. The subdued and confused four-year-old all too often develops into the angry and aggressive fourteen-year-old.

By fourteen, Kelly was in care. Her early life was not only filled with the neglect that is inevitable when a parent's primary relationship is with a drug, she also had to witness terrible acts of violence. Derek Benson repeatedly abused Jacqui. He had an unpredictable and excessive need to control his partner. Jacqui's sister witnessed one outburst at her parents' home; it was Jacqui's birthday but Derek had forgotten the card that he'd brought her. He wanted her to go back and get the card but when Jacqui refused he attacked her, ripping out sections of hair and punching her in the face. Jacqui's sister said: 'Once you see Derek [angry] you'd always be shaking. His whole face would be contorted and he would almost be foaming at the mouth. It was frightening to look at. My legs would turn to jelly.'

As the years passed, Jacqui was seen regularly at hospital A&E units. She suffered broken ribs, extensive bruising and there can be little doubt that she feared for her life. Her brother-in-law intervened during one beating and Derek produced a knife from his back pocket – he threatened to use it should her brother-in-law ever intercede again. Kelly was not immune from her father's outbursts either. In 1993, aged only six years old, she was assessed in St Claire's Unit of Temple Street Children's Hospital. Kelly and her mother were living under a reign of terror and systematic abuse. So why hadn't Jacqui left Derek, if not to protect herself then to protect Kelly?

As with many victims of domestic abuse, Jacqui felt trapped and was locked into a never-ending cycle of tension, abuse, remorse and forgiveness only to find herself spooling back around to tension and abuse and so on.

Abusers are not consistently violent. They have periods of remorse and neediness, they beg for forgiveness and they swear that they will change. They can charm, be affectionate and loving, but underlying their attempts to make amends lies a mass of insecurities that emerge to trigger violent attacks. Unable to face their guilt and anxieties, the abuser lays the blame at the feet of his victim. If you hadn't been staring at that other man, if you hadn't said no when I asked you to make me some food, if you hadn't looked at me that way, this would not have happened.

Perhaps Derek had known only violence and emotional abuse but by the time he and Jacqui set up home together, the pattern was set. As well as heroin, Jacqui was addicted to Derek and imagined that the brutality would stop, that he was truly sorry and that her situation would change. She is far from alone. Irish police report that there are more than 10,000 cases of domestic violence every year. At least ten of those women will lose their lives at the hands of a violent partner. Yet every year, women stayed locked behind the confines of the abusive relationship they know is destroying them. Women's Aid in Ireland campaigns relentlessly for better funding to maintain helplines and advice centres. They are trying to give hope, to throw a lifeline to the desperate and they are trying to change attitudes towards domestic violence in the wider community.

A Department of Justice spokesperson said: 'It is also a sad fact that many people know of women who are living with this fear, yet they choose to turn a blind eye and treat it as a private matter. Domestic violence is not a private matter. It is a matter which should be of concern to all members of society and one in which everyone can play a role in bringing [it] to an end.' But

Women's Aid and other charities know how far society is from that commitment; too many women have met indifference from the police and the judiciary. Perhaps it is no more than an anecdote but it is said that one organisation even supplies extra handkerchiefs when one judge sits as he is dismissive when listening to accounts of domestic violence.

If women often feel defeated and helpless when trapped in abusive relationships, the impact of violence on their children is yet more bleak. It is not uncommon for girls to grow up in violent homes only to form relationships with violent men. In addition, boys who grow up watching their mothers being beaten by a partner are more likely to become abusers themselves. They watch, they learn, they have no experience other than being witness to desperate and destructive role models.

Not all children go on to repeat the mistakes their parents make. Many vow never to put their children through the grief they suffered. But it will take the intervention of an outsider to break the cycle. A relative, perhaps a grandparent who can offer unconditional love, or a teacher, a consistent influence that can nurture a fragile confidence. Someone needs to step in. Someone needs to show the damaged child that there is another way to live. Who would help Kelly?

By nine years old, Kelly knew too much. She knew everything that was needed about drugs, about the paraphernalia required to inject heroin and even how to pull scams to raise more cash for the next hit. Derek had coerced her into selling fake drugs, putting her in harm's way on the streets so he could rustle up some money, money that he would spend on himself. He encouraged Kelly to smoke dope and before too long got her to help him inject.

He had no sense that he should be trying to shield his daughter from his worst excesses and instead was slowly edging her towards sharing his addictions to the full. Jacqui was aware of what was happening and tried to object but her interventions were laughed at. If she pushed too hard, she'd be beaten – and worse. Jacqui would tell the court that Derek repeatedly raped her, and that Kelly was often a witness.

It became clear to Jacqui that she could never escape Derek and that he was determined to ruin Kelly's life, as he had ruined hers. She had no confidence in the police. She did not believe her family could protect her, her own father was dying and she knew that Derek had threatened her brother-in-law with a knife. She also knew that out of all women killed by abusive partners, the majority died once they had walked out on the family home. If I can't have you, abusive men often reason, then no one will. What could Jacqui do?

The solution, when it came to her, was to have a catastrophic effect on the one person she claimed to care for – Kelly. Jacqui decided that if she could not walk out of Derek's life, she would hire someone to get rid of him. It seems implausible that she could ever imagine that this was a plan that could ever have a positive outcome but by this stage Jacqui was beyond reasoned thinking. She did not believe that Derek would ever let her live her life without him – unless he was dead.

Her first attempt ended in farce. Jacqui met 'a man from Northern Ireland' and he convinced her that he could arrange to have Derek shot for a sum of £500. She later admitted to police that she paid the man but that her would-be assassin 'fucked off with the money'.

As she endured yet more suffering at the hands of Derek Benson, she thought she'd hit on a new and ingenious plan. Another man she'd met said he could arrange to give Derek a 'bad dose of gear (heroin)'. Jacqui agreed to pay but that was as far as the scheme went. It seemed that she was destined to fail in her plan to dispose of Derek just as she had failed in every other aspect of her life ... but something changed. She found a sympathetic ear in Paul Hopkins and this time it would be different.

Paul knew Jacqui and Derek, he knew all about the beatings that Jacqui took and he didn't like it one bit. Hopkins worked as a doorman at a local pub and heard Derek boast that he'd 'cut people up', and as time passed, his dislike grew. It reached a tipping point when he heard that Derek had verbally threatened his girlfriend and their baby daughter when he was away. He'd crossed a line – what kind of man would threaten another man's girlfriend and child? In Hopkins's eyes, Derek was a violent lowlife and a scrounger. In 2000, he saw Jacqui walking down the high street in tears and he just knew Derek Benson would be the reason for her misery.

Jacqui's mother had been dead for some time and she had temporarily left Derek to care for her terminally ill father. After he'd died, Jacqui saw this as a chance to break from Derek. She was still living in her parents' house and hoped that she could stay, perhaps the small inheritance her father left her would allow her to stand on her own two feet. But she wasn't the only one thinking about the inheritance – so was Derek.

In the street that day, Jacqui broke down and told Paul Hopkins everything, that Derek had taken a bracelet from her that her father had left her in his will and that he was demanding a cut of the sale of the property – money that she knew he'd spend on drugs. It was really simple. Derek had to go. Jacqui could see no other way out. She could offer Hopkins a substantial payment, £3,000 to £5,000 – money from the house if she could sell it. She handed over a down payment of £200 to show that she was serious. Hopkins quipped that he'd have been willing to do it voluntarily. They had a deal.

Hopkins began to plan. He was a much younger man, thirteen years Derek's junior, but reasoned that he would need a weapon. He bought a sword from his brother for £50. He then bought a mobile phone and some sleeping tablets. Derek would die at home, but it would be with Jacqui's help.

Jacqui knew Derek was due to have some much needed dental work and the plan was to administer sleeping tablets once he was home at his flat and in bed. She would then phone Hopkins to say when Derek was sedated and he'd carry out the rest.

The call came and Hopkins set off, the sword concealed in a bag. Jacqui let Hopkins into the flat and he entered the bedroom where Derek was sleeping. He swung the sword down onto Derek but the sleeping man leapt up, shocked but fully aware that he was fighting for his life. Hopkins was pushed into panic by Derek's attempts to defend himself but rather than stop he worked himself into a frenzy. Derek suffered over sixty defence wounds as he tried to grapple the sword from Hopkins. In total, Hopkins inflicted twenty-five serious stab wounds, including seven that indicated that the sword was pushed through Derek's trunk completely, from his front to his back, and from his back to his front.

The attack was ferocious. When Derek ceased struggling, Hopkins surveyed the carnage around him and hesitated. It was a hellish scene and he decided to set fire to the bed and wardrobe, in part to destroy the evidence, in part to attempt to wipe the scene from his mind.

He was only partially successful as neighbours soon smelt fumes and saw smoke rising and so called the fire service at around three a.m. They extinguished the fire and in doing so found the bloodied remains of Derek Benson. A murder enquiry was launched.

It must be said that although some effort went into planning the killing, no thought went into evading justice. Detectives start every murder enquiry with a review of the victim's personal circumstances and one name came to immediate attention – Jacqui Noble. She was the long-suffering partner of Derek Benson, a woman who was frequently and violently attacked and someone who'd recently come into some money.

It took very little time to build a picture of Benson, Noble and their habits. It took only days before Paul Hopkins was brought in for questioning and for the sword, the murder weapon, to be found in the wardrobe of a friend's house. 'She said if I did it, she'd pay me,' Hopkins simply said, and both he and Jacqui were charged with murder.

What fourteen-year-old Kelly felt was unknown. Overnight, she had lost a father and a mother and she was taken into care. Could it not have ended another way? She knew all about her father's brutality, she had been on the receiving end of many beatings and had to watch assaults on her mother, perhaps the hardest thing to endure of all. But she would never have wished for it to end in more violence, and never have wanted her mother to be taken away. It seemed that, once more, her mother had failed to put her daughter first and now she was truly alone.

Yet is was not for long, Jacqui was not held on remand before sentencing – she was allowed to set up a new home with her daughter and Kelly was afforded the opportunity to make positive changes to her life. At first glance, the chances of Kelly turning her life around seemed slim, after all she was now the product of a victim-turned-killer and a tyrant-turned-victim. Two drug addicts. Two people who had failed her. But Jacqui wanted a different life for her daughter now they were free from Derek's abuse. She reached out to social services, the Garda and her family and hoped that it was not too late for Kelly. In 2002 they secured social housing in Seaview in Laytown and some element of stability entered Kelly's life but the adjustment came too late. She was an angry young woman and she squandered her chance to put her past behind her. One other factor seemed to stymie any hope of change. Kelly fell in love.

Kelly fell for an addict with convictions for robbery, arson, attempted robbery and criminal damage. This was a destructive relationship and by the time she was nineteen, she was a mum of two young toddlers, Jasmine and Leon.

Jacqui began her life sentence in 2004 and Kelly was alone again. Her life was far from easy but her temperament could make matters worse, she was known to have a sharp tongue and would not back down when confronted. Kelly's upbringing was marred by violence and it would seem that her father's legacy ran deep.

The ill-feeling between Emma and Kelly had built up over the last few years. Emma had not reported Kelly to the Garda after an argument between them became physical when Emma was pregnant. Emma knew a number of gardai personally and would chat to officers, she was trying to get her life onto a firmer footing through the juvenile liaison scheme but it is likely that she felt an argument with Kelly Noble should not involve the police. For Emma and Kelly, threats and violence bubbled below the surface of everyday life. 'Saving face' mattered but Emma may not have realised that for Kelly, violence was not accidental. She had learned that it was used by the strong to dominate the weak and Kelly did not want to end up as the weak ever again.

On the afternoon of 2 June 2006, Niamh was spending time at Kelly's flat. She'd offered to braid Niamh's hair as a birthday present, the children were with her and it looked to be an unremarkable afternoon. As the evening drew in, Kelly strapped Leon into his buggy and said she'd pick up a few things from Pat's supermarket. Walking the aisles, she had no idea that Emma McLoughlin had entered the store.

Emma was in good spirits, she was an amiable drinker, and she wasn't drunk – her blood alcohol levels would later be shown to be just over the legal driving limit – yet when she saw Kelly something flared up within her. She confronted Kelly stood behind Leon's buggy, and her voice, repeating the same sentence over and over, began to rise: 'Why did you kick me in the stomach when I was pregnant?' Her behaviour fits the profile of many young adults with ADHD, the repetition of phrases, the inability to rein in emotion or appreciate what impact inappropriate behaviour can have on others.

A store worker noted the time – it was about nine ten p.m. – and he and his colleague walked over to the two women and tried to break the altercation up. He noticed that Kelly's nose was bleeding and gave her a tissue. Emma would not stop, she continued to rail against Kelly, asking over and over again, why did you kick me in the stomach? Emma was incensed and was eventually led to the exit. But she wasn't going any further. She was waiting for Kelly to leave.

This was the point that Kelly made a choice, and it was a fatal one. She could have called the Garda or asked the supermarket staff to do so on her behalf, she could have called a taxi or simply backed down and asked for Emma to leave her alone. Shona attempted to calm her sister down knowing that her anger would subside, it always did. But Kelly called

Niamh, who was only 500 yards away and told her to bring a knife.

Niamh did, believing that her friend's life was under threat and that a knife would prove a deterrent. She got Jasmine ready to leave and walked to the store. Outside, a group of children were talking about the fight and told Niamh not to go inside. But she did and she saw Kelly holding the tissue to her bloodied face. Kelly asked if she'd brought the knife, Niamh pointed to the bag she was holding and Kelly slipped it over the handles of Leon's buggy. She then hid the knife up her sleeve.

As they made their way out, they saw Emma waiting. Niamh later told the court what she saw: 'Kelly and Emma started to shout at each other and the children started to cry. I was trying to get the children to calm down and not be looking at the two women.' She then heard a loud thud and Kelly grabbed Leon's buggy and began to stride away, Niamh following, gripping Jasmine's hand. She took one look back. She saw Emma McLoughlin lying on the pavement.

Niamh had not seen Kelly take the knife from the school bag and did not see her friend plunge it into Emma's chest. She swore that she only handed over the weapon because she thought it would cause Emma to back off, that it would defuse, not escalate the row.

It took no more than moments to end the three years of enmity between the two and it happened so quickly that even the women standing next to Emma and Kelly did not understand what had happened. Shona, Emma's sister, said: 'I didn't see the knife. When she took it out it was full of blood and I knew she was after stabbing Emma.' By then, it was too late.

Kelly was arrested and pleaded guilty to manslaughter but entered mitigation of provocation and self-defence. The idea that she reacted only in a moment of self-defence was torn apart in court in 2007. First, after the initial altercation inside the store, Kelly told a member of staff that she would 'slice up' Emma. Second, and most damning, was the call to Niamh and request for a weapon. This pointed to premeditation, a moment's planning that made her actions murder.

Why, with access to a phone, had she not called the Garda if she was in fear of her life? Here, we see an eerie echo of her mother's thought processes. Jacqui had tried to rid herself of Derek through legal channels and a barring order was placed on Derek in 1997, something he simply ignored. She lost faith with the authorities and it didn't even cross Kelly's mind that the police could be called out to protect her. During the first brutal fourteen years of her life, few had intervened; by twenty, they were not on her radar even when she felt in mortal danger.

When the news broke that a mother and daughter were both murderers, many speculated how it was possible. Looking deeper into Kelly's past, it became clear that such a dysfunctional background was a breeding ground for the worst behaviour. And yet in the actions of 2 June, we see more of Derek Benson than perhaps we do of Jacqui Noble.

Jacqui floundered from one plan to another until she found, in Paul Hopkins, a man willing to kill Derek. She administered the sleeping tablets and so there is little doubt that she was guilty of premeditated murder. Women who kill their violent partners usually snap in a moment of desperation, the knife picked up in self-defence, an abrupt fight back despite little sign of defiance having existed before. This is not what happened to Jacqui. She spent time mulling over the end of Derek Benson and on the night that she let Paul Hopkins into the flat, he asked her if she was sure she really wanted to do it. 'I was trying to get out of it. She said she was.'

When Emma confronted Kelly, she would have heard echoes of her father's violent outbursts. She took a stand. In the cold light of day, it was an unjustifiable stand, just as it always had been when Derek took a 'stand' against any sign of dissension he saw in his partner and child. When Kelly raised her hand, the blade ready to strike, it was a rage her father would have recognised.

The moment Kelly was led away to face the start of her sentence for manslaughter, four children were left orphaned; Jasmine, Leon, Jack and Holly face growing up without a mother, just as Kelly had. Although she loved her children, her decision to call for a knife on 2 June left four more children to struggle without a family home. She wrote to the McLoughlin family and said: 'If I could change going to the shop that night, believe me I would have changed it long ago. I'm so sorry the way this has ended. I wish that night never happened.'

The McLoughlins were too grief-stricken to accept Kelly's letter of apology and rejected it. Emma McLoughlin needlessly lost her life but so much more was lost that evening in Laytown. Violence destroys families and it is children that suffer most – Kelly knew that. When she held her kitchen knife in her hand, she held the lives of four young children in balance. She may believe that she acted in self-defence but in the minutes that ticked before she left the store, she allowed all that was dark in her life to triumph.

CHAPTER FIVE

Margaret James
Tainted Love

The coward's weapon, poison
John Fletcher

Villages such as Mylor are defined by the sea. Shipping may no longer be the main source of employment but boats still outnumber residents by three to one. Not all the boats are large, some are only used for leisure, others take tourists sea fishing for the day but a few, like the *Clairvoyant*, are fishing vessels. Perhaps it was just as well that it was the *Clairvoyant* that spotted the half-naked body of a man floating towards them one June morning in 2004 – it is not quite what tourists expect to see.

Reaction on the boat was calm. It is not uncommon for fishing boats to encounter the bodies of drowned sailors, surfers or canoeists. The crew of two knew what to do: they would pull the dead body aboard and report the find to the coastguard and police. Using a grappling hook, it was hauled up onto the deck and straight away the fishermen thought that this was an unusual drowning. The head of what looked like a older man had four deep gashes in it. There were other injuries too and the crew wondered if it was possible that they could have been caused by a collision with a boat's motor. The men noted its location, about five miles south-east of Black Head, off the Lizard peninsula, and in doing so, they helped uncover one of the most extraordinary murders the area had known.

Once ashore, the body was removed for post-mortem. The police checked missing persons reports but drew a blank. The post-mortem would take place the following day, Saturday 19 June, and it quickly became clear that this had been no boating accident. The man, who seemed to be in his late fifties or early sixties, had suffered eighteen separate injuries, including four deep cuts to the head, the likely result of blows from an axe or machete.

Other injuries included broken ribs, a broken kneecap, severe bruising to his chest and back, a severed big toe and grazing to the man's buttocks. This last injury was significant as it suggested that the body had been dragged across hard ground. All in all, these injuries were not consistent with anything that could have happened at sea. There was also evidence of a high quantity of sedative in his system and the pathologist made one further observation: the man had not been dead when he hit the water. The final cause of death was from drowning and the police, led by Detective Inspector Neil Best, knew they now faced a murder enquiry.

At first, the police only announced that there were 'unexplained' injuries on the body. By Monday the twenty-first they had learnt that the man was 56-year-old Peter Solheim, a resident of nearby Carnkie and a parish councillor. An incident room had been set up but the police were cautious in their approach as they needed to establish as much information as possible about Mr Solheim and his movements up to 18 June, the day he was found by the *Clairvoyant*.

The police were told that Solheim had a girlfriend, 56-year-old Margaret James. She lived outside the village of Porthoustock, in a remote former coastguard's cottage. She would have to be told that Mr Solheim had been discovered and hopefully she could fill in the blanks about his final few hours. Margaret was able tell them about her last meeting with Peter but it wasn't quite what the two detectives expected to hear.

Margaret said that she last saw Peter when she drove him to Mylor Harbour on 16 June, two days before his body was discovered some thirteen miles away at sea. He was setting out on a boating trip and was meeting up with a friend called Charlie. Asked why she had not reported him missing, Margaret said it was because she expected him to stay out at sea for some time so was not unduly alarmed. Peter Solheim did have a boat but not one equipped for overnight fishing. It was a twelve-foot dinghy, the *Izzwizz*. Again, Margaret mentioned Charlie – she believed that he had a bigger boat and that the two men planned to use it for a long fishing trip, to France or Spain.

Who was Charlie? Margaret had no details other than she thought he was an old friend of Peter's. She had no contact number, no surname and, in truth, the detectives who spoke with her found her manner oddly impassive. She had been informed that her boyfriend of some eight or nine years had been found dead after suffering several unexplained injuries but she was composed, unperturbed even.

No two reactions to a sudden death are the same but experienced detectives can read subtle signs in the behaviour of a victim's family and friends. It remains true, after all, that most victims know their killers. No one is above suspicion and Margaret James, with her vague recollection of events, names, times and an apparent indifference to her boyfriend's suffering, raised doubts that she was telling officers all she knew.

A prime suspect often emerges in the first few hours of a murder investigation. As the police build a picture of a victim's life, details of disagreements, disputes and ill-feeling surface; all breeding grounds for murder. Margaret James was now under suspicion but as the police dug into the background of councillor Solheim, they were to uncover a life so unconventional that it was possible that any number of people could have wished him ill. They would learn that the sleepy villages of Cornwall were also the backdrop for black magic, drugs, sex, firearms and explosive rage. Nothing was as it first appeared.

Peter Solheim grew up on the outskirts of Falmouth, the only son of a Cornish woman and a Norwegian sailor. His father, a chief engineer on a whaling ship, was often away and Peter was raised almost wholly by his mother. He did learn to sail but did not want to follow his father's footsteps and work at sea, instead he had a number of jobs inland, working as a panel beater, in a printing works and various jobs where he used his skills to fix machinery. In 1971 he married Jean Poley, a clerk, and they went on to have two children: a girl, Lisa and four years later, a boy, Daniel. In many ways, his life was unremarkable, but that was all set to change.

His daughter would later say that after her parents divorced, Peter Solheim became a changed man. As someone who'd always struggled to contain his temper, Solheim began to show symptoms of manic depression. His relationship with his children had never been easy but after one argument he told a neighbour, 'I don't care if I see nothing of them the rest of my life.' If Solheim found his failed marriage difficult to cope with, his decision to sever relations with his children in the mid-nineties would prove catastrophic. Casting off his past, he was free to explore the more extreme aspects of his personality. They would coalesce into two obsessions; sex and witchcraft.

Outlets for these twin obsessions were benign at first. Feeling rejected after the breakdown of his marriage, he sought solace in the arms of other women and would regularly reply to lonely hearts advertisements. His involvement in the occult began as little more than an interest in Cornwall's landscape and ancient past. But Solheim had a fatal flaw that ran through his psyche: enough was never enough. No matter how many women he seduced, no matter how many pagan rituals he attended, he always wanted more. He was never satisfied and as, over time, his behaviour became increasingly extreme, he found himself in a world that embraced anything, even murder.

Margaret James was unaware of Solheim's struggles when they met in 1995. He'd replied to a lonely hearts ad she had placed and he turned up at her home with a bunch of flowers. She was flattered by his attention. It was a welcome distraction for Margaret as she had something of a tragic past. Her husband died in the mid-1980s when the bus he was sleeping in to save money whilst working at a gravel pit caught fire.

Margaret had raised their two children alone. It was an insurance payout that arrived some years later that allowed her to buy a coastguard's cottage in Cornwall.

At first, her circumstances inspired a degree of sympathy in local residents yet it did not take long before many started to see her as something of an eccentric. It wasn't because she was a vegan or that she embraced paganism, swimming naked or walking barefoot in all weathers – anyone is entitled to their beliefs no matter how off-centre – what concerned some was that Margaret had little desire to 'fit in' and many disapproved of the manner in which she kept her home – some even claimed it was 'filthy'.

Not everyone held this view. Margaret was seen to take good care of her elderly mother, had good relations with her daughter and doted on her grandchildren but there was a side to her personality that few saw and as details of her alternative lifestyle emerged, it shocked even those locals who had their doubts about the 'hippy' grandmother.

When Margaret met Solheim, the two were in their late forties. At first, Margaret was delighted by the ardent nature of their relationship. She was candid with the police, telling them that they were 'at it like rabbits'. This was more than the first flush of passion at the outset of a new romance, Peter Solheim was insatiable and Margaret would come to learn before too long that she was not the only object of her boyfriend's passion.

Women who find that their partners are unfaithful have a choice. Some turn a blind eye, though they are few in number and usually have other concerns such as keeping the family unit intact. The majority make a clear ultimatum: if they cheat, they go. There is a third route, women who are comfortable with the dynamics of 'open relationships'. Margaret seemed to oscillate between all three and in doing so caused herself a good deal of unhappiness.

She tried to stay in step with Solheim's interests, in the hope that it would help their relationship. Soon she joined Solheim as he attended rituals and celebrations, all of which were harmless. There is an active, if small, number of people fascinated with pre-Christian spirituality who find alternative ways to appreciate and embrace nature. Paganism attracts the curious and the open-minded, and the vast majority have nine-to-five jobs and secure home lives. Some, however, are less stable. One druid would later comment that Peter was 'definitely veering towards the dark side of magic'. He was drifting from an interest in paganism towards Norse gods and, more specifically, was excited about their promise of 'power'. Whilst it was common to wear white robes to ceremonies, Solheim began to don a horned helmet, breastplate and sword and asked to be called 'Thor's Hammer'.

If Solheim was drifting off the scale in his eccentric approach to spirituality, it was noticed that a small figure was almost constantly at his side. Margaret seemed very proud of Peter and the only moments of obvious discomfort came when she had to watch him flirt openly with other worshippers. Peter did not hold back. He would make lewd remarks and boasted of his sexual conquests. In truth, he was never going to be the best looking man in the room and his sense of sexual potency often made other women laugh. It was possibly an aspect of his manic depression, experiencing a 'manic' episode, he believed nothing was beyond his reach, whether it be women or channelling Thor.

Margaret tried to appear relaxed about his sexual promiscuity, she tried to free herself of society's norms that placed restraints on sexuality and she tried to be free in body and in mind. But it was in vain. Her anger, when it erupted, was without limits. She spied on Solheim, broke into his home, told a friend that she'd discovered women's underwear as 'trophies' in his attic, along with a voodoo doll and potions, and she was frequently agitated when discussing him. Yet all this evident distress did not stop her continuing the relationship; it was almost as if she could not help herself.

Perhaps self-esteem was an issue. Solheim could charm and no doubt he was capable of convincing Margaret that she was the prime relationship in his life. Yet he was open about his other habits and they alone should have given Margaret good reason to end this destructive relationship. By the time he took up with

Margaret, Solheim was living on disability allowance, unable to work because of his manic depression and yet he earned money, a good deal of it, by trading in antique firearms and pornography. But Margaret hung on to Solheim, even as the stakes grew higher and higher.

Peter Solheim did more than boast, he did have several relationships with other women and there was one that he'd return to again and again. Jean Knowles had been married three times and her liaisons with Solheim stretched over a period of twenty years. She would later admit that near the end of Solheim's life, they would meet to have sex on average three to four times a month, something that Margaret was expected to put up with. Eventually the two women would clash and Margaret would warn Jean to stay away from Solheim, but the on-off affair continued regardless.

If Margaret knew that Solheim was capable of lying to her, she also knew that he was capable of terrifying flashes of temper. Several neighbours in his village of Carnkie had run-ins with him. The house he renamed Valhalla had a shared access drive and if a parked car blocked it even slightly, Solheim would lose his temper and barricade the car with his own. He dumped coal outside one garage during one dispute, fired air guns in his garden, shone a torch into one house, repeatedly complained of noise and announced he was videotaping his neighbours' activities. The police were contacted over his intimidatory tactics and they advised caution when dealing with him. At one stage they did call at his property but that was after a tip-off that he was holding illegal weaponry. As well as guns, Solheim had an interest in knives. The police found quite a hoard of antique weapons and he was cautioned as some were unlicensed.

Yet during this time, Solheim was an active parish councillor, somewhat at odds with his image as a hell-raising wiccan. His spiritual beliefs informed his work as a councillor and he had a passion for the environment. The downside was immediately obvious. He had a virulent dislike of 'outsiders', even if residents had lived in the area for three decades, they would never be 'Cornish' in his eyes. He also gave vent to his more outlandish views, claiming that floods were a result of angering 'river spirits'. Margaret even joined him on one occasion, walking barefoot as he inspected a proposed development site. As many of the covens he'd joined had asked him to leave, it can only be wondered how long the parish would have put up with his more eccentric behaviour and views.

If his temper and his promiscuity were not enough to drive Margaret away, what kept her at his side? One theory is that she relied on the money Solheim generated through his various activities and it would be a theory presented as a motive for Solheim's murder at her trial. The picture was somewhat more complex, yet

Margaret's finances and attitude to money do reveal a key insight to her character.

Margaret earned near to nothing herself and, on paper, she relied on a monthly £327 widow's pension and council tax benefits. Once the police began to dig into her finances they found a quite different picture, however. She had an ISA worth just over £7,000, some £71,725 invested in her daughter Lucy's name, £650 worth of premium bonds, £15,270 in a National Savings investment account, a £12,564 capital bond plus £671 in a dormant account in Barclays. In truth, Margaret hoarded cash and she knew Solheim did too. He was often flush through selling antique weapons and pornography. It was even said that Margaret once found £900 hidden in a book at Solheim's house. As they were leaving, she pretended to Solheim that she'd forgotten a purse and went back in, took the money, hid it in her skirt and left a fanlight open to make it look like a possible burglary should her boyfriend notice the cash had gone missing.

This was a far from healthy relationship and by 2001, Margaret was actively researching poisons and noting the quantities needed to prove fatal in humans. Magic played a role too – she devised potions and incantations in the hope perhaps that happiness would be hers once more. But six years is a long time to endure misery and dissatisfaction. Something would snap in the end. Something would force Margaret to act decisively and when it came, as she feared, it was something that was completely out of her hands. Peter fell in love.

An odd romance in many respects, after twenty years of dalliance with the 61-year-old Jean Knowles, Peter decided it was with her his future lay. By 2003, Peter would regularly stay overnight with Jean, he asked for her hand in marriage and even began to renovate his mother's old house, telling her that it would be their marital home. Jean knew about Margaret. Margaret knew about Jean. A difficult situation and one that Jean managed with more ease than the younger Margaret. Perhaps because she was in the ascendant, perhaps because her expectations of Solheim had never been clouded by false hope, yet when Solheim bought her an engagement ring at the end of 2003, Jean sensed that this time his break from Margaret would be permanent.

Solheim was no fool. He asked Jean not to wear the ring, not yet; he still had to extricate himself from his entanglement with Margaret and was wary about how she would react. Yet even he, self-proclaimed master of the 'dark side', had little idea how gruesome the end would be.

The police would later search Solheim's home where they noticed a calendar complete with an entry for 15 June 2004. It read: 'Secret's found out.' The following day Margaret told the police she'd taken Solheim to

Mylor so that he could sail out and meet Charlie. There were no sightings of Solheim after the sixteenth. The police would be left with many puzzles to solve after Solheim was found floating off Lizard Point on the eighteenth and the 'secret' would be just one of them. Was the secret Solheim's engagement to Jean Knowles? Could it have meant that Margaret had discovered that their relationship was at an end and did it trigger an act of terrible revenge?

At first, Margaret was just one possible suspect; who, for example, was Charlie? Could Solheim, who was believed to have dabbled in drugs, have been smuggling contraband into Cornwall from Spain? Could he have crossed the wrong person in one of his attempts to use black magic? He had boasted in the past that he was capable of being a good friend but made a 'very bad enemy'. Perhaps his sense of omnipotence backfired. Perhaps he'd pushed the patience of a neighbour too far and someone had snapped. But then something was uncovered that would switch the focus of the investigation entirely. Solheim was sending text messages.

At least that was how it was supposed to appear. Both Margaret and Jean Knowles received texts from Solheim *after* 16 June. They supported Margaret's account of events as they confirmed that he was on his way to meet Charlie. The police made several requests that Charlie, or anyone who knew who this 'Charlie' could be, come forward. Not only were locals unable to help,

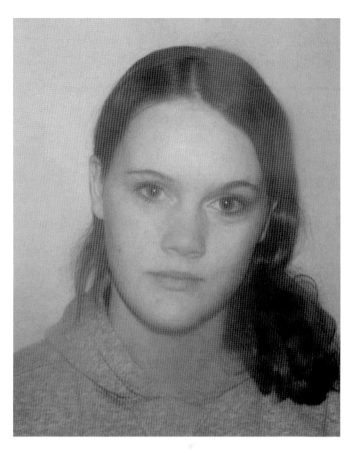

1. Sixteen-year-old Chelsea O'Mahoney, a gang member whose night of 'happy slapping' attacks left one man dead.

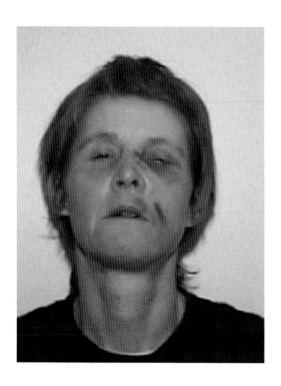

2 & 3. Therapist Heather Stephenson-Snell photographed after her arrest. Police also took pictures of the 'Scream' mask and weaponry found in her car.

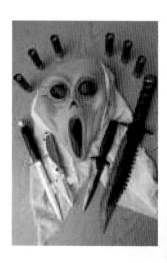

4. The House of Blood killers. From left to right, Edith McAlinden, her 16-year-old son John and his friend Jamie Gray.

5. Louise Gardner believed that Rachel Jones had broken a window at her mother's house. Later that day, Rachel was pulled from her bicycle and killed in a frenzied knife attack.

6. In 2004, Kelly Noble's mother was jailed for the murder of her father. Three years later, Kelly would also be imprisoned after stabbing to death a mother of two.

* Picture credit: Collins Photo Agency

7. The 'Scissor Sisters', Linda and Charlotte Mulhall. The two killed their mother's boyfriend then mutilated and dismembered his body in one of Ireland's most gruesome murders.
* Picture credit: Collins Photo Agency

8. Margaret James with her lover Peter Solheim. His drugged and bludgeoned body was found floating off the Cornish coast.

9. Rose Broadley standing with Robert Butchart. Broadley was believed to have thrown a prostitute to her death from a Glasgow tower block and was convicted of murder. The conviction was later quashed on appeal.

* Picture credit: Mirrorpix

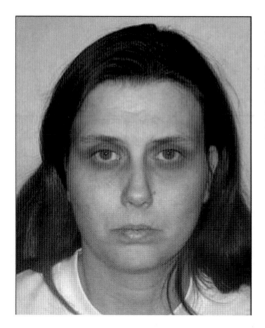

10. Cheating wife Maria Boyne, killed her husband in a brutal and sustained attack. She hoped his death would clear the way to moving her lover into the family home.

11. Tracey Connelly, mother of Baby 'P'. Peter's identity was initially concealed along with those of his tormentors.

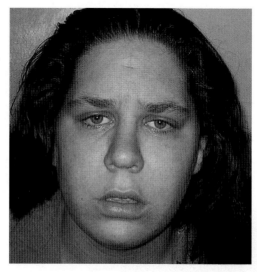

they also noted wryly that in their part of the world 'going to see Charlie' was a similar euphemism to 'going to see a man about a horse', a phrase used to hide what you were really up to.

But if the texts were designed to push the police to step up their search for Charlie, they badly misfired as Jean Knowles didn't hesitate to tell them that they could not have come from Peter Solheim.

The texts sent to Jean referred to 'Margaret'. When talking or texting Jean, Solheim never used Margaret's full name, always calling her 'M' and as their relationship fell apart, even referring to his girlfriend of nine years as 'it'. This was not enough for the police to act on but it did at least raise the possibility that the texts may have been sent by someone other than Solheim. Proof, when it arrived shortly afterwards, was conclusive. Cheery texts were still arriving even though Solheim's body was in the morgue.

The police traced the texts and found they were indeed being issued from Solheim's mobile but they were being sent from on land, through the St Keverne transmission mast, the closest one to Margaret's mother's home.

Margaret stuck doggedly to her story and yet the facts were painting a very different picture. The pathologist raised the possibility that Solheim had been kept somewhere on land prior to death, as the marks on the back of his body suggested that he'd been dragged across rough ground or gravel. It was possible that he was held somewhere for up to two days before being dumped, badly injured, into the sea.

Adding to the confusion surrounding the true sequence of events was the discovery of Solehim's boat, the *Izzwizz*. It was found lodged between the pontoons in Mylor Harbour, the key still in the ignition. The coastguard were tasked with establishing if it was possible for Solheim to fall out of his dinghy and then float out to sea, some thirteen miles away. Programming that monitored the tides proved that was impossible, as was the chance that the dinghy could have drifted back into the harbour after an accident at sea. That left two possibilities: either Solheim had been transferred to another boat or someone returned the *Izzwizz* to the harbour after he had been dumped. The police wondered if it was possible for the diminutive Margaret James to carry out such a feat alone.

The police interviewed those who knew Margaret and that included her daughter's ex-partner who was also the father of her daughter's two children. He admitted to detectives that Margaret had been unhappy with her relationship with Solheim for some time. Margaret had even asked her ex-son-in-law if he knew anyone who could 'get rid' of Solheim, some three years before Solheim disappeared.

Modern policing demands that detectives proceed with caution when putting together a case. The role of the police is not to find a suspect guilty, it is only to establish the facts. Once the decision is made to arrest and charge a suspect, the investigation enters an entirely new arena. The suspect will have legal representation, there to protect the interests of their client. Once the case is ready, it is forwarded to the Crown Prosecution Service (CPS), an independent body, which makes the decision as to whether the case will proceed to trial. If it does proceed, it will be because the CPS believes it has a good chance of ending in a successful prosecution.

The drawbacks to the system are immediately obvious. Whilst it makes sense for the CPS to assess each case on its merits and not clog up the courts with ill-thought-out or weak prosecutions, the danger is that marginal cases will be set aside. Rape cases are typical, as they often boil down to one person's word against another and a jury can struggle to reach a verdict that is 'beyond reasonable doubt'. The fear is that if the system is allowed to drift away from prosecuting difficult cases, justice will not be served. The fear is justified in certain respects – across England and Wales, for example, only 6 per cent of reported rapes result in convictions.

The police in the Peter Solheim enquiry knew that the evidence suggested that Margaret James had an involvement in his murder but it would take some time before she was charged. The hope was that it would become possible to identify who else was involved. In that, the police were to be frustrated.

Other evidence incriminating Margaret was gradually uncovered. Solheim was known to have a small fortune in cash at his home. He had a safe but it was missing from his home and only twenty pounds or so was found at the property. Margaret, who was not working, had £900 under her mattress. There was a note wrapped around the cash: 'what go (sic) around, comes around.' This could be thought of as circumstantial and as Solheim was known to have many thousands of pounds in cash, some wondered if the money had been paid out to a hired killer. But the money, close to £24,000, did turn up, under a house in the nearby village of Helston. The house belonged to Margaret's mother.

A compelling case pointing to Margaret's involvement had been built but no other names had appeared in the frame. The charge, when in came in February 2005, was for murder and conspiracy to murder. For the prosecution, it made sense to build on the evidence; the texts sent from Solheim's phone from Margaret James's home, the cash found at her and her mother's houses, the bitter end of their relationship, Jean Knowles's statement that Solheim feared that Margaret would react badly, and her enquiry to her ex-son-in-law about ridding herself of Solheim. Yet the prosecution also knew that it would be difficult to state without doubt that Margaret was the killer, that it was she who drugged him, she who struck the fatal blow and she who tipped her lover out of a boat.

The trial at Truro Crown Court in early 2006 attracted nationwide attention. It seemed improbable that a retired parish councillor in his late fifties could have led such a double life and yet more revelations were to emerge during the trial. An expert in paganism and witchcraft testified that Solheim did keep ingredients for spell making and potions in his attic. Professor Hutton said that the range was 'extraordinarily large and impressive' and was the basis for spells designed to lure the opposite sex and to curse any enemies.

It also came out that the 'quiet grandmother' had written to her son, who was in prison, naming men who might beat up Solheim. Stanley Reeves, her ex-son-in-law, also revealed that she had visited him to ask if he knew someone who would kill Solheim and how much it would cost. She also discussed poison with Mr Reeves, saying that she hoped to find something to sprinkle in Solheim's food without it tasting of anything. Asked why he didn't contact the police, Mr Reeves said that, although he thought Margaret was serious, he thought it best to just warn Solheim. Even then, Mr Reeves didn't mention murder, just that Margaret was looking for accomplices to beat him up.

After Mr Reeves and Margaret's daughter ended their relationship, he maintained contact with Margaret and she often visited her granddaughters. He also noted that after Solheim's body was found, she showed no remorse.

No one in court could have imagined that the lives of a grandmother and a parish councillor could have been so complex and dark. Whatever the truth of Solheim's final hours, only a few things are clear. Solheim was poisoned. High quantities of Lorazepam, a powerful sedative, were found in his system. It would be difficult to imagine Solheim being forced to take the drug by a stranger, it is far easier to imagine him having ingested it during a meal. Once drugged, he was removed and held, possibly for up to forty-eight hours. He was savagely beaten and a ring that Jean Knowles had given him, and that he was wearing during his final weeks, had been torn from his finger. He was transferred to a boat that dumped him, still conscious, at sea.

Margaret remained silent. The judge at the trial faced a dilemma. Margaret could have been present at each stage of Solheim's poisoning, imprisonment and torture but the evidence presented to the jury had not proved conclusively that she was. Midway through the trial, Judge Graham Cottle told the jury: 'The prosecution, in order to succeed, have to prove either that the defendant alone murdered Solheim or that she played an actual part in his murder. There is, in my judgement, and it is my judgement as a matter of law, insufficient evidence for either of these conclusions safely to be drawn.

'It therefore follows that when you are returning your verdict on the conspiracy charge you will on my direction return a verdict of not guilty in relation to the charge of murder. Hereafter you will be considering the conspiracy charge alone.'

This could have proved a fatal blow to the prosecution but fortunately, in British law, a conspiracy to murder can also carry a life sentence. Four weeks later, the jury retired to consider its verdict. The following day, the foremen stood and informed the judge that they had found Margaret James guilty of plotting to kill Peter Solheim.

Judge Graham Cottle imposed a sentence of twenty years and in his summary said: 'It was you who wanted him dead and you who masterminded and orchestrated the events which culminated in his death. I have no doubt at all that the arrangement for his abduction, torture and disposal were of your making. And what you orchestrated was a horrific and slow death.'

The judge went on to add an insight of his own. He said: 'I have had an extensive opportunity to observe you during this trial which has lasted over ten weeks. I have had the opportunity to see you give evidence and heard from you over a period of several days – you are a consummate actress, the performance demonstrated your ability to lie with apparent conviction but clearly you experience no remorse for what you did.'

His view was more than a condemnation, it was a

revelation. Margaret James was capable of being all things to all people. The good daughter chatting over a fence to her mother's neighbour, the pagan worshipper, the kind grandmother, the drug user, the widow, the potion maker and the vengeful spurned lover. In Peter Solheim she may have believed that she had found a new love but she only succeeded in finding a man who would bring the darkness in her to the surface.

Solheim was always seeking a new high, a new spiritual revelation and all he uncovered was the destructive payback for his selfish behaviour. In those final few hours, he saw the real Margaret. He would have seen that she was not a woman he could shake off or set aside now that he no longer wanted her. The irony is that Margaret James would not be able to rid herself of Solheim either. When his body was dumped off Lizard Point, it was with the intention that it would never be found. It was fate, a fluke or luck that brought it floating into the path of the aptly named *Clairvoyant*. And for all the pagan rituals attended, all the magic potions imbibed, neither one of them saw how their story would end.

Devon and Cornwall Police are still hunting the accomplices they believe aided Margaret James. The case is not closed, but Margaret will know that more than anyone.

CHAPTER SIX

Louise Gardner
The Blood Feud

*While seeking revenge, dig two graves – one for
yourself*

Reverend Dr Douglas Horton

When it came, it came quickly. The girl, who looked
no older than sixteen, was pushed off her pink mountain bike and punched. She screamed 'Get off, get off,'
but was kicked, punched, stamped on, and then came
the knife. She was on her back when the first blow was
made to her chest, then her face was slashed. It was a
short but frenzied attack and the killer simply walked
away, towards a car which drove off, leaving behind a
scene of horror.

The whole event was witnessed. It had been an unremarkable early evening in March 2008 and the streets

around the closely packed estate in the Anfield area of Liverpool were still busy as teenagers milled around talking together. One group saw the attack from the very start. The girl on the pink mountain bike had cycled up Whitefield Road, a car behind her. The car, a black Fiat Punto, stopped and one of the passengers got out, a women with long blonde hair. She shouted out to the teenagers: 'Girls, grab her for me!' The group of friends looked on, unsure what was happening – was this a robbery?

The girl on the bike cycled quickly and turned into Woodville Terrace, the blonde-haired woman running after her shouting: 'I'm going to kill you.' As she ran, the teenagers followed; this was too good to miss. It was in Woodville Terrace that the cyclist was caught, trapped. One of the teenagers, a boy of only fifteen, saw the knife, saw the kicks and punches, saw the gouges made in the face of the girl as she lay on her back, her chest and the back of her head punctured with stab wounds. He later told the police: 'She tried to lift her head up, but she couldn't.'

The group of teens were in shock as the woman walked away and some of the girls began to cry. There was panic; it was hard to see the girl's face through the slashes and bruises and it was hard to tell if she was even alive. A few seconds later, Elizabeth Blanchard heard the commotion. A grandmother and local resident, she came out onto the street when her daughter ran to her shouting: 'There's a girl, I think she's dead.'

Elizabeth pushed her way through the crowd that had gathered and saw the girl lying motionless. There was no response when she lifted her chin and gently pinched her ear but Elizabeth had the presence of mind to move her into the recovery position on her right-hand side. An ambulance had been called and someone in the crowd handed Elizabeth a phone; it was a call handler at the emergency services who wanted to talk her through CPR (cardiopulmonary resuscitation).

Of course, call handlers cannot see what is happening at the scene but are trained to instruct callers to attempt a resuscitation as prompt action in the first few minutes can mean the difference between life and death. Elizabeth checked the girl's airways and tried mouth-to-mouth resuscitation. It was a desperate scene – Elizabeth could not know it but the girl's jaw had been broken in the attack; it was impossible to tell from the blood loss caused from stab marks across the girl's face.

It was hopeless. Some of the fourteen stab wounds had punctured the girl's heart and her life had slipped away. The ambulance arrived and Elizabeth was helped to her feet. She was thanked as she stood covered in the blood of a girl no one knew.

The police were at Woodville Terrace within minutes

and the scene was sealed. Detective Sergeant Mark Baker, a police officer of many years standing, was shocked by the scale of violence the girl had suffered. It was one of the most horrific incidents he had attended. The task of interviewing witnesses and carrying out door-to-door enquiries began as did the search for the murder weapon. The girl had been taken to the Royal Liverpool Hospital but was pronounced dead on arrival, at this early stage, it was still not clear who she was.

As the next twenty-four hours unfolded, the police worked tirelessly to establish the identity of the victim and trace the blonde-haired woman who had carried out the attack. It became known that the victim was not a teenage girl but a woman aged twenty-six. It surprised those who'd seen her that day as she looked young in her tracksuit and trainers with her hair tied up. Identification had proved difficult. The victim carried nothing to indicate who she was and it took vital hours for the police to piece together a name and address. Eventually, they were able to find an address for the victim's mother, Mavis Jones. Breaking the news to relatives that a loved one has been killed is one of the hardest tasks in policing. Mrs Jones could not take in what the officers at her home were telling her – it seemed impossible – but despite her rising panic she had the presence of mind to ask: 'Where is the baby?'

With the address now known, officers called to the woman's flat. No one came to the door so police forced an entry. They noticed that the curtains were still drawn. In one of the rooms there was a cot. One of the officers looked into the cot and found a baby lying on her back gazing up at the ceiling in the darkened room. The infant had been left alone for twenty hours but happily she was in good health.

The victim was named as Rachel Jones. She was not originally from Liverpool but from nearby Chester and had lived in the area for seven years or so. There was shock and sadness amongst Anfield residents. Some had been concerned that local drug-dealers were damaging the character of the once close-knit community yet Rachel Jones's death was not the result of a drugs dispute, nor was it a case of road-rage that ended in violence – this was an act of bloody revenge.

The police soon tracked down the driver and passengers of the black Fiat Punto. As initial statements were gathered at the scene, witnesses told the police that the blonde woman had shouted about a broken window. Checks were made to see if any reports had come through involving a smashed window in the area and, sure enough, one had. It led to a woman about the same age as the victim, a 25-year-old called Louise Gardner. She was living with her mother, Diane, in Mallow Road, a street less than a mile from the cul-de-sac where Rachel Jones had lost her life.

A search of the route the car would have taken if it had travelled from Woodville Terrace back to Mallow Road was undertaken and Louise Gardner was taken into custody. As it was a Saturday, she was held until Monday morning when she was taken to the Magistrates Court to be charged with murder. Like Rachel, Louise was a mother and it seemed incredible that she chased a woman down, trapped her and took her life in a frenzied attack. What could have happened to provoke such fury and blood lust? A broken window, it seemed. Louise said that Rachel had broken a window and that it was the final straw.

Rachel had a twin sister Becky and she told the police that there was a history of ill-feeling between the two women and that the attack should not be thought of as an isolated incident. But for the detectives involved with the case, a broken window could not account for such an extreme attack.

The more Becky talked about the past, the clearer the picture became. This was a feud that had its roots in a disagreement that stretched back over seven years and at that stage, Louise was not even involved. The catalyst of it all was Louise's younger sister, Vicky.

Becky told the police that after her sister moved from Chester she had been befriended by Vicky. The girls were then both in their late teens and Rachel was pleased to make a friend so soon after arriving in the city with her newborn daughter, Demi-Lee. Rachel's relationship with Demi-Lee's father had not been easy – this was a classic 'on/off' affair that hadn't been easy for Rachel and now she had full-time responsibility for their child, she felt that life in new surroundings might offer a fresh start. Vicky seemed like a antidote to her worries as she was full of life and enjoyed partying.

Before too long, however, Rachel grew wary of Vicky. She thought that Vicky was caught up in a crowd that used other people's houses as impromptu venues for parties. Rachel moved house; uncertain that she could trust Vicky and her friends, at the back of her mind was the worry that any promises of a few quiet drinks would soon be broken.

Once one of these parties was under way, it would be joined by any number of people texted or called and the flat would be overrun. What concerned Rachel was the fear that a party could get out of hand, that there would be a huge mess to clear away and that if any serious damage occurred amongst the partygoers, half of whom Rachel would not be able to name, she would be left to pick up the bill. She was hardly in a position to pay for repairs and losing her deposit would be a nightmare.

The situation came to a head when Rachel heard that some of the Franey family were now hanging around. The name Franey will mean little to those outside Liverpool and perhaps not even to those outside Kensington, the area where Rachel and Vicky were living. A large family, some of the Franeys had become notorious. Daniel Franey was thirteen years old in 2001 when he was made subject to an ASBO (an antisocial behaviour order). To secure the order, evidence was presented of persistent offences stretching back over four years that included smashing windows, racist abuse, making threats to kill and throwing bottles.

In 2002, fourteen-year-old Darren Franey, along with two other friends, were chased by police as they headed back from Chester towards Liverpool in two stolen Vauxhall Vectras. Darren was behind the wheel of one of the cars as it sped into the Kingsway Tunnel, under the Mersey. The tactics police employed to slow the vehicles are still a matter of controversy. A heavy goods lorry was moved across into another lane and Franey, travelling at over 100 miles per hour, was unable to swerve past it. He crashed and was killed along with his fourteen-year-old friend Scott Veach.

Five Merseyside police officers were suspended over the incident but were later told that they would not face criminal charges. This was a huge disappointment to the Franey family but by then they had fresh concerns to contend with. Operation Turbo was an undercover operation focusing on stolen cars. The police opened a bogus garage called Clearance Car Corner and installed surveillance equipment. Over a sixteen-month operation, they recovered over one million pounds' worth of stolen cars and £300,000 worth of illegal drugs. Eighteen-year-old Damon Franey was one of the men filmed delivering stolen cars, and two of his other brothers, Liam and Gavin, had also been involved in the investigation but were both serving jail terms by the time Damon received his 200 hours of community service order.

Gavin Franey had made the headlines but not just for Operation Turbo. In 2001 he had robbed a post office in North Wales, terrifying the sub-postmistress by holding her around the throat and shoving her into a wall, even though she was holding a baby. On a day release pass in October 2003, he absconded and went on the run. The police advised that should any member of the public spot Gavin, they should not approach him.

The Franeys were well known in and around Kensington although there is no evidence that they had been at parties held in Rachel's house. It was rumoured that Vicky's older sister Louise was seeing one of the family but Rachel gave it no more thought.

In 2001, with Demi-Lee aged one, Rachel returned to Chester to stay with her mother. She was away only a matter of a couple of days but it was long enough for some of Vicky's acquaintances to turn up at the flat, kick the door in and turn the place upside down.

Rachel felt betrayed. She felt particularly vulnerable as a mother and even though it is doubtful that Vicky could have held back those intent on using the flat as a party house that night, Rachel blamed her friend. It should be remembered that Rachel was young, only nineteen years old, with an infant to care for and the flat was her harbour from the outside world. She felt it had been violated, and with no one to turn to the anger she felt towards Vicky began to fester.

Many teenage girls who find themselves pregnant and with little hope that their boyfriends will stay the course, dream that motherhood will become a source of solace and joy. For most it is, but every mother learns that the care of a newborn also brings moments of exhaustion, fear and frustration. Raising a child places huge demands on any woman's emotional resources and without support young mothers can sink under the weight of expectation and despair. There is nothing that can undermine a mother's sense of self quite like an inconsolable infant.

Worries about the ability to provide care can give way to self-loathing or, in some cases, irrational rage at the actions, real or otherwise, of others. It is a defence in some ways, to prevent a corrosive self-doubt settling into depression. There is no let-up in motherhood, no days off or hours of uninterrupted rest, you have to keep going and externalising anger can be a way to keep physical and mental collapse at bay.

In the long hours of the early morning, Rachel thought about how Vicky let her down. How could Vicky have let them kick in her door and destroy her flat when she knew she had to bring Demi-Lee back here?

A few months later, Rachel spotted Vicky as she was shopping and the two began to argue. Harsh words led to blows being exchanged and Rachel's anger now escalated into a long-term enmity. Once it had become clear to Vicky that her ex-friend would not accept an apology and could not forget what had happened between them, it was inevitable that her sister would find out. Louise was protective of her sister and was unsettled by the fact that her younger sister was hit by a still-irate Rachel months after the party. She would not stand for it.

Families naturally pull together if there is an external threat, loyalty is to a great extent natural, but it is a gut instinct that often clouds judgement. An impartial observer would have been able to see that Rachel did have a grievance and that by taking sides and denying that she had would only inflame matters. One voice of reason was Rachel's twin sister Becky who urged Rachel to move on and focus instead on Demi-Lee. Becky admired the way Rachel cared for her daughter and hoped that would be enough to distract her sister from her feud with Vicky Gardner. But it wasn't to be.

At first, life appeared to have pushed the bad blood aside but even in large cities communities can feel as small and oppressive as a village. Everyone knew everyone's business in Kensington and walking into familiar faces day after day meant that ill-feeling was constantly stirred up. Louise would not back down when it came to looking after her sister's interests and if you made an enemy of Vicky, you would of the whole family. Safety in numbers usually ensured that a spat went no further but it isn't always the case. Sometimes, it drags an entire family into a spiral of futile violence.

Why Rachel could not let the matter go is not clear. Like many women in tougher urban neighbourhoods, she felt that if she was seen to be a pushover, her life could only become more perilous. It is better to fight your corner and be seen as someone not to mess with than be seen as a lightweight to be taken advantage of. The problem is, what starts as defending your corner can turn into a war of attrition that can never be won.

Perhaps the situation would have died down but Louise, who was usually flanked by a group of friends when she went out, would see Rachel out shopping with Demi-Lee and would shout, laugh and taunt her. It sabotaged Rachel's attempts to put the incident where it belonged – in the past.

Demi-Lee turned five years old and with a place at school, Rachel could have broadened her horizons, thought about leaving the area or started afresh through work or retraining. Instead, she found herself involved with Demi-Lee's father once more and before too long found that she was expecting a second baby. Sadly, once again, it seemed that her relationship was not going to work out.

Alone once more, Rachel coped as best she could when her second daughter, Atalia, was born but she could have had little idea that she would not see her new daughter's second birthday. The feud with the Gardners had flared up again – she had an argument in the street with Louise and the only thing that stopped it turning physical was the fact that she was pushing Atalia in her pram. Rachel was unable to shake off the incident; it was as if all the ill-feeling from years earlier was fresh again in her mind. She demanded a 'straightener' with Louise, determined to bring matters to a head.

This was a volatile situation and yet no one could believe that the two women, both mothers of young children, would escalate their dislike of each other up a notch. But one person was near breaking point – Rachel.

Becky had pleaded with her twin to drop the whole matter. She could see the toll that it was taking on her sister and she was worried. Becky did not know that Daniel Edge, the new man in Rachel's life, was similarly concerned and when Rachel raved that she would show the Gardners that she could not be intimated, he tried to warn her that it could only get worse unless she backed off. 'I don't care if I get stabbed,' Rachel said but even then, Daniel thought that her words were only bravado.

It is likely that Rachel did not fully appreciate where the next few months would lead her, that her act of defiance would trigger a dreadful endgame that would leave her two girls effectively orphaned.

First, someone threw paint stripper at the Gardners' car. Louise wondered if Rachel Jones was responsible. Next, someone threw paint at the house. This time, Louise guessed that this was no random act of vandalism and believed that the home she shared with her mother had been targeted. On one hand, Louise's belief that it was Rachel was logical. Despite the years that had passed, Rachel could not forget that her home had been attacked. It was the one place she and her daughters should feel safe and Vicky had allowed it to be wrecked. An attack on the Gardner home would be an obvious revenge. See how they felt.

However, Louise had fallen out with more people in the area than Rachel. Perhaps this was the work of someone else with a grudge. If, however, it was Rachel, and if she hoped that Vicky would then understand what it meant to have your property and belongings targeted, she had not allowed for how outrage could manifest itself. It may have caused Rachel years of resentment, but in someone else the reaction was entirely unpredictable.

*　　*　　*

If Rachel was behind the acts of vandalism, perhaps all the powerlessness she had felt when she returned home with baby Demi-Lee in her arms to find her flat had been wrecked had been banished by an act of revenge. Perhaps, for a few hours, she felt a rush of control. Perhaps that is why she got on her bike on the early evening of 14 March 2008, cycled to the Gardner house and threw a brick, shattering a window. She was spotted near the house, the hood of her top pulled down, laughing. A report was made to the police. But that wasn't enough for Louise.

It was totally out of character for Rachel to leave Atalia. Demi-Lee was staying elsewhere for the night and Becky knew her sister to be a devoted mother and the risk she faced by leaving her daughter unattended remains inexplicable to her family. She left with just her house key and a pound in her pocket. It was as if she was popping out for a pint of milk and yet she was spotted near the Gardners' home, laughing. The brick had not only smashed the window, it had caused a moment of genuine terror.

Of course, at this point the Gardners could have told the police of their suspicions and let them handle it. They could have trusted that Rachel would come to her senses. This time, as Rachel was seen cycling away, they could have provided the police with an identification and explain that they suspected this was an ongoing campaign of retribution over a very old disagreement.

Rachel would have been questioned and with so much at stake, namely her children, she could have been forced to snap out of her need to fight back.

No one was hurt at the Gardners' home, just badly shaken by the broken window and the realisation that someone could have been caught by the brick or glass. Enough was enough, this madness between Rachel Jones and their family had to end. But Louise did not pick up the phone. Louise picked up a knife and she got in her family car. She was going to hunt Rachel down.

It is important to remember that Louise was not alone in the car. Together, they had a fair idea where Rachel would head – back home. They knew the route she'd taken. The first few minutes of the pursuit surely should have been enough time for them to cool heads and ask themselves what on earth they were doing, chasing down a lone mother. Minutes ticked by. No one stopped the chase. Louise has since spoken of 'the madness' that took hold of her.

Rachel was fleeing for her life. Everywhere she cycled, the car would soon hove into view. Eventually, Louise left the car to chase Rachel on foot but she was close to losing her. Her account of what followed makes chilling reading. She said: 'I just switched. I was just knackered running and I could not breathe, and then I have done that with a knife and got all the energy. I could not stop it. I can just remember stabbing her in the chest and then in her face. I took hold of her hair and then I slashed her face ... I knew where I had stabbed her with the knife, but I could not control what I was doing. Nothing was stopping me. It was like my body did not want to stop.'

The attack on Rachel was devastating. The first blow was to the back of Rachel's head and was followed by repeated attacks as she was dragged from the bike by her hair. As well as being stabbed fourteen times, her jaw was so badly shattered that had she survived she would have been permanently disfigured. Louise repeatedly stamped on Rachel's head, a particularly brutal and inhumane gesture that far exceeded any offence caused over a broken window. Louise was hate itself.

Many of us can understand anger, have felt moments of rage and intense dislike over the hurtful actions of others, yet very, very few of us will reduce another human being to an object to be savaged beyond recognition. As Rachel tried to raise her gouged head, her life ebbing away, she would have heard, as the gathering crowd did, Louise Gardner laugh as she walked off.

It took the police very little time to piece together who the protagonists were in this brutal affair. Within fourteen hours, Louise Gardner had been arrested and charged with murder. Hers was hardly a sophisticated attempt to evade justice, all that followed was a series of denials and prevarications.

Louise said that she was provoked by Rachel, and no

doubt to an extent she was. She said that it was Rachel who held the knife and that it somehow fell into her hands and that she used it in self-defence. This notion was undermined as the police had searched the Gardner home and found a box for the distinctive Crosscut lock knife lying behind the microwave. It is an unusual knife with a difficult opening and closing mechanism.

The detectives interviewing Louise allowed her to elaborate on her story – namely that it was Rachel who carried the knife. They asked Louise what she did with the weapon once the attack had ended. Louise admitted that she had thrown the knife down a roadside drain and it was quickly recovered. One detail was immediately noted – the knife had been closed.

Some of Louise's evasions were designed to protect others, such as her friend Elizabeth Kerwin. When asked where her bloodstained clothing was, Louise said that she'd dumped them in a wheelie bin. An extensive search was carried out but in fact the clothes were recovered from Ms Kerwin's house. She told the police that Louise had turned up at her door about an hour after the attack and handed her the clothes in a plastic bag. Louise told her that she'd been in a fight but did not know what had become of the other woman. Elizabeth Kerwin hid the clothes under her stairs, never imagining that they were the clothes of a killer.

Floral tributes were laid at the site where Rachel Jones lost her life and the community tried to understand what could have provoked such a bloody end. Rachel's family were devastated and Becky's heart broke each time Atalia greeted her as if she were her mother, not her aunt. As the trial date approached, they had still not come to terms with their loss but hoped that a guilty verdict would allow them to secure a measure of justice for Rachel. As the jury filed back into Liverpool Crown Court on 8 September 2008, both families were shocked. The jury had failed to reach a verdict.

The prosecution immediately stated that they would proceed to a retrial. For the police, it was a disappointing outcome. They had done all that was necessary to provide the Crown Prosecution Service with a water-tight case and yet there was something that troubled the jury, the idea that Louise was sufficiently provoked.

The notion of 'reasonable force' has long been used as a guideline by the law in the UK as juries accept that if an individual is under attack, defending oneself, even with considerable violence, is lawful. It is not a hard-and-fast rule but is intended to have a wide degree of flexibility as each case has to be judged on its merits. Juries will take into account age, physical fitness and the nature of the threat and use common sense to assess what is a reasonable use of force.

So, for example, if a woman was alone at home with her children and a male intruder broke into the house brandishing a weapon and the mother smashed a torch over his head causing a fatal injury, the force used would be seen to be justified. In fact, in cases such as this, it would be unlikely that the Crown Prosecution Service would prosecute.

It is in fact very rare for a householder to be prosecuted, less than one a year, and yet when they do, the story is often highly controversial. Cases such as that of Norfolk farmer Tony Martin who shot and killed sixteen-year-old burglar Fred Barras. Martin was jailed for life in 2000 but his sentence was reduced to manslaughter on appeal in 2001. The police took no satisfaction from the case but as Barras was shot in the back with an illegal hand-held shotgun, they had to act.

It was a very divisive case and stirred up a good deal of emotion amongst those who have lost faith in policing, in the criminal justice system and who fear that they are powerless to defend themselves against the 'rising tide' of criminality. It is doubtful that these were the thoughts that provoked Louise Gardner to seek her revenge rather than call the police. What motivated her seemed far more primitive and yet a symptom of the age – selfish individualism.

The Joseph Rowntree Foundation carried out extensive research into social attitudes in 2008 and it seems that most of us are aware of and unhappy at the rise of the 'selfish citizen'. The Foundation's Director Julia Unwin said: 'From the public consultation we did last year, there was a strong sense that the decline of community has corresponded with a rise in individualism. Participants suggested that people increasingly look after their own individual or family interests without considering the needs of society or the community.'

There exists more than one generation today that puts their own interests first; they believe their emotional needs matter more than those of anyone else, they demand 'respect' even if it comes at the cost of the humiliation of others and they are aware of their 'rights' but rarely their responsibilities. This is the rise of the teenager on the bus shouting abuse and throwing chips at passengers, the woman who screams obscenities at the old man who asks her not to drop litter, the father kicked to death for not giving a teenager a light.

This twisted self-absorption has led to number of disturbing and excessively violent outcomes, just as it did on a March night in Liverpool. Both Rachel Jones and Louise Gardner felt aggrieved, both had a claim to feel upset, but neither could step back and defuse their rage. Rachel did not deserve her fate, Louise carried out a hideous attack provoked not by a broken window but by a distorted filter where only her emotions were considered, no one else's. It was a narcissistic orgy of violence that was in every way unjustifiable.

The retrial opened in February 2009 at Liverpool Crown Court and after two weeks of argument, the jury retired to consider its verdict. The police were anxious not only for Rachel's family but for the young witnesses who had seen the attack. Many were traumatised by what they had seen and they had to relive the events of the evening once more. The prosecution stressed two key pieces of evidence uncovered by the initial investigation. First, the discovery of the Crosscut knife box at the Gardner home, undermining the notion that it had been Rachel who had carried the weapon. Second, once the knife had been recovered, it had been found closed. The prosecution argued that the lock knife required a degree of familiarity to open and close it. Was it plausible that Louise Gardner had grappled it from Rachel Jones and then encountered no difficulty in closing the blade?

This time it took only one hour for the verdict to be reached. Louise Gardner remained impassive when she heard the word 'Guilty' and maintained her composure even as Judge Gerald Clifton sentenced her to life with a minimum term of sixteen years. He said: 'You have shown not one particle of remorse. You ended the life of a young woman and deprived two very young children of their mother.' Louise waved and smiled to her family as she was taken away.

In allowing herself to be led by her sense of outrage, Louise deprived her own child of a mother too. Two families were left bereft and evermore divided. During her post-mortem, it was noted that Rachel had the names of her two daughters tattooed onto her hip and ankle. It was a small sign of her devotion to the girls. Two women, two mothers, who lost all they had in one night. Yet in today's climate of heightened self-inter-est, it is doubtful that they will be the last.

CHAPTER SEVEN

Charlotte and Linda Mulhall
The Scissor Sisters

The line separating good and evil passes not
through states ... nor between political parties
either – but right through every human heart
Alexander Solzhenitsyn

When a picture from a mobile phone was leaked to the press in Dublin in August 2008 there was huge public outcry. At first glance, it was fairly innocuous, just a picture of a man in a baseball cap holding a birthday cake and to his left, a young woman larking around by holding a large knife to his neck. It is only when it was realised that the woman was Charlotte Mulhall, serving a life sentence in Mountjoy jail, that the picture took on a sick and sinister meaning.

Mulhall, one of the 'Scissor Sisters', used a knife to

dismember a man in 2005. She also used a hammer and brute force, for as Charlotte and her sister Linda now know, it takes a huge effort to tear a man apart limb from limb. If you don't have the right tools to hand, it will take hours.

Charlotte's decision to fool around and hold the knife to a male inmate's neck triggered a review of security arrangements at the prison and soon afterwards she was removed to another secure unit in Limerick. That left Linda behind in Mountjoy, something Charlotte regretted as the two relied on each other – they always had. Since their incarceration in 2006, they'd spent their time learning hairdressing skills, card making and basket weaving. It's good to have skills to fall back on and the two had spoken of their plans to work as beauticians one day. That day is still some way off.

How much is each of us a product of our environment? It is a question that did not tax the District Detective Unit that led the investigation into the torso found in the Royal Canal at Ballybough Bridge in Dublin on 21 March 2005. Their minds were focused on the task ahead – to find out who the dead man was, how he died and who was responsible. Standing at the canal's edge, with the towering Croke Park stadium in the background, the gardaí sensed this was no ordinary murder. They were right but what would surprise all involved were the ordinary characters of the killers.

Charlotte and Linda Mulhall were not career criminals and although they'd been in a few scrapes they were not known to the police as violent offenders. Linda had a conviction for a charge of larceny way back in 1993 and although Charlotte had run up some public order offences, they were relatively minor and a consequence of drunken episodes. Charlotte knew how to drink but as one in three Irish people admitted that they regularly binge drink, placing them at the head of the survey for the European Union, Charlotte's excessive drinking was not particularly notable.

Indeed, Charlotte had been brought up in a climate where using alcohol to escape day-to-day life was the norm. Her father, John, had been a heavy drinker and his family had borne the brunt of his temper in the past. He had beaten Charlotte's mother Kathleen on several occasions and although his character calmed as the years passed, Charlotte and her siblings had seen what damage alcohol abuse can bring to a home. By 2005, Kathleen and John were no longer together but it would soon emerge that Kathleen had jumped out of the frying pan and into the fire.

The family home was in Fettercairn, a large housing estate in Tallaght, at the foot of the Dublin Mountains. Tallaght is only eight miles south-west of Dublin and its proximity meant that a once quiet rural village changed beyond recognition after the 1960s as it became subsumed by the City. Rapid development and construction of a vast shopping centre served some of the residents well but not those deposited in Fettercairn in the 1980s.

For an estate with a population of over 6,000 the community is poorly served. There are no GPs' surgeries, no dentists or pharmacies but the health of the residents is affected by more than a lack of a health centre. Unemployment and school drop-out rates are high, one in five families is headed by a lone parent and unplanned pregnancies are common. As well as a lack of opportunities, the estate is troubled by antisocial behaviour with burnt-out cars, graffiti and boarded-up and vacant houses all contributing to a sense of despair.

Residents claim that they are reluctant to call the Garda if they see criminal incidents for fear of reprisal. That may be no more than a perception but it adds to the high level of stress many of the locals feel.

Residents have also complained that regular blasting from the nearby Roadstone quarry can coat the estate in a fine dust and question whether it has added to the high number of respiratory complaints in Fettercairn. It is a bleak picture and a less than ideal environment in which to raise children. John and Kathleen Mulhall had tried their best and by 2005, their daughter Linda had also four of her own to raise.

Linda lived at the family home with her young children as none of her relationships had worked out. Both she and her children had been on the receiving end of several beatings from the men in her life. Being back at home with her father seemed the best option and although Linda adored her children, she could not shake off the need to use drugs and alcohol to obliterate her anxieties.

Casual use of drugs, such as ecstasy, had become the norm for many in Linda's generation. The idea of stepping outside your life for a few hours of drug-induced oblivion was seen as no bad thing. Life on the poverty line is a punishing blend of monotony and stress so the temptation to escape by bingeing can be a strong one. As well as the depressing reality of life with a lack of prospects, living at the family home in Kilclare Gardens was not without its complications. A year or so earlier, Kathleen Mulhall had met someone. A man who was not only much younger but from Somalia; or at least that's where he said he was from.

Kathleen was besotted with the tall and athletic Farah Swaleh Noor and made the bizarre decision to move him into the family home, right under John's nose. Their marriage had run its course but this was asking too much of her husband and so he moved out. Yet within a year he was back as Kathleen and Noor had moved on. It was a complicated set of relationships but the Mulhall children made the best they could of it, deciding to remain on good terms with both their parents.

John helped out with babysitting Linda's kids when

he could as did Marie, another sister who lived in the house. Kathleen had recently moved back to Dublin with Noor – into a rented cottage in Ballybough, which lies to the north of the city – after some months in Cork. She had taken the ground floor flat at No 17 Richmond Cottages, in a Victorian two-up two-down terraced row. Noor had signed on for casual work with the recruitment agency and Kathleen had organised benefit payments for them both. It wasn't much of a life but it was all Kathleen wanted: to be with Noor, or at least to be with him when he was sober.

Noor can't have failed to remind Kathleen of John Mulhall in his younger days. When sober, he was the perfect gentleman, easy company and sociable to all he knew. With drink inside him, a switch would flip and he'd let his demons control him. He was aggressive, domineering and would lash out. Kathleen was not the only woman to learn of this dark side to his nature. Before they'd met, he'd courted a young girl from Cork and they'd moved in together.

At first, all was well but his drinking started to ruin their relationship. Noor became increasingly violent, abusive and domineering, slowly starving her of time with her family and friends. He was a classic domestic abuser, first isolating his girlfriend and then terrorising her into submission. She became pregnant and they had a baby son and, although he adored the baby, his use of violence increased.

His need to dominate took a devastating turn and he began to use rape as a humiliating way to subdue his girlfriend. A broken woman, her family finally learnt that she was a virtual prisoner and with Noor away, managed to rescue both mother and child.

It isn't known what Noor felt about the end of this relationship. He harboured a deep and abiding violent impulse in his dealings with women but was also given to maudlin self-pity, crying over the loss of his son, and in a drunken stupor he often imagined he saw the young child walking around the streets of Dublin.

Kathleen knew about Noor's son and she soon came to learn more about his temper. She was beaten by him several times and yet never chose to end the relationship. Perhaps she believed Noor's apologies when he sobered up, and hoped he could change, yet she cannot have failed to notice the distress on her daughters' faces when they saw her argue with Noor. It would always start with something minor but it would build into a full-blown rage and both of them would use their fists. Theirs was a volatile affair but it was about to take a turn that neither could have foreseen.

It all started so well. St Patrick's Day weekend with the sun out and the streets of Dublin swarming with crowds looking to celebrate and relax. Charlotte knew the city would be the place to be so she asked Linda if she'd travel the few miles into Dublin with her and meet up with their mum and Noor. Linda wasn't sure if she was up to it, she found life with the kids demanded most of her energy and it would not be easy to get a babysitter at such short notice. Perhaps it was meant to be, though, because their father walked in and said he'd be happy to mind the children.

The two sisters got themselves ready for an afternoon and evening out. They started drinking vodka as they chatted and put on make-up. To look at, the sisters shared physical similarities and yet were very different. Linda was fair-haired and quite slight when stood next to her taller and stockier dark-haired younger sister. What they shared were distinctive and slightly hooded eyes. Both had plucked eyebrows they'd redrawn in a sharp line, both used kohl to heavily outline their eyes in black. It gave them a severe, even menacing look, although it was unintentional.

They were meeting up with Kathleen and Noor outside McDonald's on Upper O'Connell Street. The street was heaving with crowds but the atmosphere was high-spirited. Everyone wanted to have a good time.

Linda saw Kathleen and motioned to Charlotte. Both looked across, as many did, at the sight of their middle-aged mother holding hands with a man substantially younger than she was. Noor was used to being the object of interest ever since he first arrived in Ireland seeking asylum almost ten years earlier. Black faces were not plentiful in Ireland until fairly recently and as the economy grew in leaps and bounds and parts of the developing world collapsed deeper into warfare, corruption and extreme poverty, more and more immigrants reached the shore of the Emerald Isle.

Despite a reputation for friendliness and with its own history of economic migration, refugees in Ireland have suffered from racially motivated attacks. An Amnesty Irish Section survey revealed that 79 per cent of migrants had experienced racist abuse as the economic boom saw major shifts in communities as the non-indigenous population grew from 1 per cent in the late 1990s to over 12 per cent a decade later. Noor was part of the shifting make-up of modern Ireland and, standing on O'Connell Street that afternoon, he was perhaps hoping to show his allegiance by wearing his Ireland football top.

Noor had arrived in Ireland late in December 1996 and lodged his appeal for asylum in January 1997. His story mirrored many of those from war-torn parts of Africa, desperately seeking shelter in the West. Except, Noor wasn't who he claimed to be at all, he was not fleeing Mogadishu, the blighted capital of Somalia, and his family had not been slaughtered in the civil war that engulfed the country; they were safe in Kenya, Noor's true country of origin. He had left behind a family that wondered what had happened to Sheilila Salim – Noor's real name.

What had happened was that the man seeking his fortune in the West had found little but low pay, hard work and limited prospects. This was not the land 'paved with gold' that Noor had imagined. He had known hard work in his lifetime – he had worked in Kismayu in Somalia, a fishing port where he'd learned to haul a catch and enough about local customs to blag his way into Ireland some years later. Once there, however, he was not looking to toil indefinitely. Noor wanted reward and part of that came through heavy drinking.

There is no doubt that Noor's drinking had worsened since his arrival in Ireland and by the time he'd met Kathleen, he was little more than a functioning alcoholic. St Patrick's Day was an excuse to get intoxicated on a day where excess would be tolerated. Noor wanted to give full vent to his frustrations with his new life and use the one substance he could rely on to extinguish how he felt. Yet in all his years of drinking, Noor was yet to learn that his efforts to drown his sorrows always ended in failure. The more he drank, the closer to the surface his rage rose. And on that March weekend in 2005, thousands of miles from home, he was indulging in his last drinking bout.

A lot of vodka was drunk on the afternoon that the Mulhall sisters met up with their mother and Noor. After walking around the streets and soaking up the atmosphere, the next port of call was the boardwalk, overlooking the River Liffey, at the heart of the city. Charlotte and Linda took the opportunity to take some ecstasy tablets and soon started a fit of giggling. It stood in sharp contrast to the mood of Kathleen and Noor who'd begun one of their arguments. The younger women zoned out, hoping the row would wind down.

As darkness began to fall, the ill-feeling between Kathleen and Noor seemed to heighten rather than dissipate and the decision was made to move off the boardwalk and head for home. Pushing their way past the revellers, Noor grabbed the shoulders of a young boy, imagining he was the child he'd left behind in Cork, and Kathleen had to pull him off.

The next sighting of Noor as he stumbled up O'Connell Street would prove vital in the weeks ahead. Dublin is a sizeable city so it was more than a coincidence that Noor should bump into Mohammed Ali Abu Bakaar, a man he'd last seen in Kismayu. Bakaar greeted Noor warmly and then advised his old work colleague that he should go home and sleep. Noor was clearly inebriated but he made great efforts to introduce his drinking companions to Bakaar.

They were but a few minutes' walk away from Richmond Cottages but the good feeling that had buoyed Noor up after his chance meeting with Bakaar had disappeared. The arguing began again.

Kathleen's flat was on the ground floor, to the front of the house. Once inside, Charlotte and Linda took more ecstasy and Kathleen decided to crush a tablet into a glass of lager she'd poured for Noor. He wasn't a recreational drug user and it will never be understood why Kathleen imagined that by spiking Noor's drink it would help improve matters but it is possible that she thought it would have the same effect it had on her two daughters, who were still laughing and sharing jokes in spite of Noor's raised tones.

If Kathleen was hoping that Noor would be artificially 'uplifted' it wasn't to be. In fact the change in his mood only matched that of his previous drinking episodes – Noor's thoughts turned to sex.

This was a problem. If Noor had singled out Kathleen, then that would have been something for the older woman to try and manage, perhaps she would have suggested that her daughters make their way home. But Kathleen was invisible to Noor – at that moment, he only had eyes for Linda.

It was an awkward moment. Linda could barely understand Noor at the best of times as she found his accent too dense to follow but his intentions needed no translation: he was tugging at Linda and trying to get her to sit on his lap. Charlotte grew irritated with Noor's persistence for good reason. Her mother was humiliated and Linda was feeling threatened. He would not keep his hands to himself and, in a drunken mumble, kept repeating that she was a 'creature of the night'. No one knew what that was supposed to mean but Kathleen began shouting at Noor.

Fuelled by drink, the row intensified. Kathleen had

pushed Noor back into the bedroom but he had grabbed Linda's waist and was refusing to let go. Charlotte screamed at him to keep his hands off her sister but Noor could not see that his refusal was a threat to Linda's safety – he saw it as a confrontation between him and Charlotte and he was never going to let a woman push him around. If he let go he was effectively backing down and his sense of male pride could not allow it. He can have had little idea how quickly the issue was spiralling out of control, even when Charlotte came out of the kitchen holding a Stanley knife, something left behind after the carpet was fitted in the bedroom he was standing in.

Charlotte held the knife up to Noor but he still would not comply. Linda was crying, her mother shouting and Charlotte did not know what to do, she just wanted Noor to get his hands off Linda. Then it happened. Charlotte thrust the Stanley blade into Noor's neck.

It might not have been enough to kill Noor but it was enough to loosen his grip on Linda. He staggered backwards in shock as blood started to splash down onto his Ireland football shirt. Kathleen's screams reached a new pitch. Charlotte panicked, there was no other way: kill him or he'll kill us all.

Linda was handed a hammer. Charlotte still held the knife in her hand. As Noor stumbled backwards into the bedroom he was savagely attacked by both women, both lost in a frenzy of rage and intent. He fell backwards, smashing his head against the bunk bed in the room, but this was only the beginning. As he was lying prone at their feet, the sisters showed Noor no mercy during a sustained attack. He was no longer a threat to the women as repeated blows to the head from the hammer wielded by Linda meant he had long ago lost consciousness, but it was still not enough to satisfy the sisters.

Charlotte left the bedroom and returned from the kitchen with a bread knife. She then set about the motionless Noor, stabbing into his flesh with so much force that she ruptured his kidneys, his liver and punctured both lungs. The hammer blows continued too and the ferocity was such that Linda left indentations on the floorboards beneath the carpet each time she missed or slipped when targeting Noor's head. The attack had obliterated his features and as exhaustion finally took hold, the women looked down on an unrecognisable and bloodied mass.

A new fear gripped them. This was no longer borne of anger at the confrontation, which now seemed to belong to another time, this was terror as the reality of their situation hit home. They had murdered a man. His mutilated corpse was at their feet. Looking at each other, they saw a mirror of their own horrific state – their clothing, limbs and hair stained with Noor's blood and shards of his flesh. What had they done?

Kathleen was hysterical; she was screaming her despair, all thoughts now for her daughters, not the man she thought she had once loved. His last word had been 'Katie', his term of endearment for Kathleen, but she could focus on only one thing. They had murdered Noor – now they had to get rid of him.

Charlotte and Linda dragged the bloodied remains of Noor into the small bathroom and sat down. They could hear Kathleen's wailing. This all had to go away, had to stop. 'We'll chop him up,' that's what Linda later told the police she heard her sister say. Charlotte denied that the suggestion was hers but by then it was hard to ever know fact from fiction, or the night terrors from the images that cascaded through her mind when awake. What neither woman denied was that their decision to dismember Noor took a very, very long time.

It is not easy, dismembering a corpse. Fred West used to take deliveries to an abattoir and became fascinated with the quick and efficient processes involved in butchering livestock. They were methods he later mimicked when disposing of the girls he and his wife Rose had tortured. Fred West had specialised tools and took his time disarticulating limbs. He set aside bones as trophies, bones that were never discovered.

Charlotte and Linda Mulhall were not serial killers as the Wests were, this was a single episode of psychotic frenzy, but once they made the decision to take Noor apart limb from limb, they entered a macabre if small group of killers whose notoriety ensured their names would never be heard without a shudder of disgust and incomprehension. Their attack on Noor may have begun as an act of self-defence but they did not repel him with a single blow or two. Once he'd hit the floor they could have phoned the Garda to ask for help.

Had Charlotte's knife wound to Noor's neck proved fatal, she would have had every opportunity to make clear that she was attempting to protect her sister. Most members of a jury would have understood that she lashed out, particularly as Noor had a history of attacking women. In fact, if the attack had stopped as it began, it is possible to imagine Charlotte Mulhall leaving court acquitted of murder.

But this was not one blow meted out in defence of a loved one. She and her sister not only killed but then acted barbarically. Alcohol and ecstasy were later blamed for their irrational impulse – it was suggested that they were caught up in a drug-induced psychosis – yet this explanation is not without its flaws. The drugs they took would have lost their potency at some point during that night but as they wore off, neither chose to address what they had begun. Both continued to take a full part in their dreadful act.

In addition, Kathleen had not taken drugs. As a mother she may well have imagined that by disposing of Noor, her daughters might get away with murder but drunkenness cannot account for her complicity in the slaughter that followed.

The women began their grim task. Hacking through

Noor's flesh, sawing with the bread knife, his muscles, sinews and tendons resisted their efforts. Sweat poured from them, their hands and arms ached and they took turns in continuing to scythe through his legs. They reached bone. Nothing they had to hand seemed to make any impact on Noor's femurs. Charlotte retrieved the hammer and began to smash down onto the white bone beneath her.

They both took more ecstasy, hoping it would boost their flagging energies. It was hard work and Charlotte's hammer blows had caused more blood and tissue matter to spray around the tiny bathroom. It was difficult to work around the body and each other. Towels were used to mop up blood and bind the legs as they slowly sliced through cartilage and bone. The towels were sodden; it was simply not possible for them to absorb the volume of blood leaving the butchered limbs.

Worse was to follow. Linda cut off Noor's penis. This had nothing to do with the purpose of disposing of a corpse, this was a gratuitous act of sexual violence. The victim turned perpetrator.

Linda would later struggle to explain why she had genitally mutilated Noor. One statement suggested that Kathleen had told Linda that Noor had raped her during their turbulent months together. Perhaps knowledge of that, along with his drunken advances on her that evening, was enough to provoke a terrible revenge. Perhaps during that long night of butchery, Noor was no longer one man but every man who'd ever hit, betrayed and attacked her. Whatever the true motivation behind Linda's decision to pick up the bread knife and saw through the dead man's penis, it was an act that stands apart from all others she participated in that night.

There was still so much to do. Charlotte thought the torso still too heavy and bulky to lift into plastic bags and so they would have to cut it in two. The upper leg bones had been removed but the lower legs were left with the feet attached. They thought they could keep the lower torso with the hips in one section and proceeded to hack through the middle to leave the upper torso as a separate section. If this was logic, it in no way took into account the gory reality of disembowelling the body. Organs and intestines spilt out onto the bathroom floor, the smell overwhelming.

The last task was to remove the head. Hours had passed, possibly as many as five, since the first knife had struck Noor. The sisters were mentally and physically exhausted and tried to keep encouraging each other as they took it in turns to rest. The head was no easy task. Linda covered what remained of Noor's features with a towel and the hammering and hacking continued. Finally, the cervical vertebrae of the neck were sawn through and the sisters were left with a body in eight separate sections.

But what now? An attempt to clear up the hell they

had created began. Some time earlier, before midnight, they had called their father John. He had to listen as his daughters cried and babbled about Noor being dead. It made little sense to him and he put it down to excessive drink. But as the minutes ticked by he began to worry. What if his girls had done something stupid?

It is significant that they called John. Kathleen no longer spoke to her ex-husband but her daughters still saw John as the man who could protect them and make everything better. But Dad would not be able to help this time. In fact, his humanity would be their undoing.

He arrived at Richmond Cottages at around one thirty a.m., just to reassure himself that it had been little more than a fight or a falling out. At first, relief flooded through him as the three women were sitting in the flat as if nothing had happened. His question was a simple one: 'Where's Noor?' John expected to hear that he'd left after a row but Linda pointed to the bedroom. He glanced in from the hallway but could see that Noor wasn't there. He walked back into the sitting room to tell the girls but this time Linda led him back and pointed to the black bin liners in the corner of the room. John still didn't understand and, confused, glanced in one. It was enough. He ran to the front door and threw up onto the pavement outside.

He told them he wanted nothing to do with what they had done. John was no lightweight, he was a tough working man who'd known his share of violence but this was beyond anything he'd encountered or could ever understand. It broke his heart. Kathleen and he may be finished but he loved his daughters dearly. Now they stood like strangers before him.

He walked away and the sisters broke down. Seeing their grotesque crime through the eyes of the father they loved was sobering and disturbing. Perhaps for the first time, they began to understand the enormity of their transgression.

Tears would not be enough. They had to act. They had already cleaned themselves up and now began to clear up signs of what had occurred that night at the flat. None of them could drive and so any plan for disposal would have to be carried out on foot. Linda suggested that they left the head behind to dispose of later. Her reasoning was plain – the body, if discovered, would be harder to identify without a head. She was right. It was left behind in a plastic bag, placed inside an old suitcase to be retrieved later from the back garden.

With body parts in sports bags, the sisters walked through the night for only a few minutes until they reached the Royal Canal, then edged their way down onto the bank under Ballybough Bridge and dumped the contents into the canal. They had to repeat the journey a number of times until all the sections were deposited into the water.

Back at the flat, the cleaning continued. It took hours, the rest of the night in fact, as Noor's blood had soaked though the bedroom carpet and onto the floorboards. The bathroom, not surprisingly, was hardest of all to clean and the scrubbing and mopping took them through until daylight.

By mid-morning the flat looked in order and the three women sat down exhausted. There was still Noor's head to dispose of and they began to debate where best to hide it. What followed next was a bizarre display of both the extraordinary and the mundane. The three women were picked up on CCTV walking through the centre of Dublin, stopping at a supermarket to buy salad rolls to eat as they window-shopped. They boarded a bus and made their way back to Tallaght as they had agreed that they would bury the head in the Sean Walsh Memorial Park – a park they all knew well.

Although they had decided that the landscaped park was the best place to deposit the head, none of them had any idea where. They walked around for some time and eventually settled on a spot only a few metres from a park bench. Charlotte dug a hole with a knife as Linda held the bag. It wasn't a deep hole but by then all three were on the verge of hysteria again and just wanted to be rid of the item as soon as possible. Kathleen then threw the knives and hammer used in the dismemberment into one of the nearby park lakes.

Kathleen returned to the flat and the sisters made

their way back to their father's house. Both felt a mix of disbelief, fatigue and fear. Once home, they burnt the bag that had transported Noor's head and began to drink once more. Neither could process what they had done and so sought to obliterate all they felt and thought.

Later that same day, Marie, another of Kathleen and John's daughters, came home from work and found Charlotte sobbing and distraught. Charlotte told her sister that she and Linda had killed Noor as he'd tried to rape Linda. She also said that they'd cut him in two and buried him near the canal. Marie could tell that Charlotte had been drinking heavily and simply did not believe her. It seemed an incredible tale but, like her father, Marie would play a crucial role in the weeks and months that followed as she came to understand that her sister's confession was not make-believe.

There followed a strange lull at the Mulhall household. With Noor disposed of, the whole episode began to feel like a terrible dream. There was no police knock at the door, John and Marie continued with their lives, so perhaps the sisters could too. It was a calm of sorts but it was not to last.

At the Royal Canal, there was the strangest of sights. Floating to the surface was what looked like the torso of a headless dummy, probably something from a clothing display that had been vandalised. It floated, however, not because it was a fibreglass mannequin but because of the air left in Noor's lungs. Pedestrians walked over the bridge, giving the torso a quizzical look but little more. A few stopped and one or two spent time looking at other objects in the water. They were each wrapped in plastic and bound with brown tape and were of different shapes and sizes. One could be an arm, another a leg.

It was the Fire Service that was summoned in the end; a call had come through on 30 March to say that a passer-by thought a body might be in the canal.

By then, Noor's remains had been in the water for ten days. When the fire crew arrived they realised this was not a call to help retrieve someone who'd fallen into the water. So they set about using a drag – a piece of equipment used to fish items from water – to pull one of the objects to the surface. No one was convinced that the item was anything other than a mannequin until it broke the surface. First, there was clearly trau-matised flesh and tissue around the break in the limb, an arm. Second, there was the overpowering stench of rotting flesh.

The limb was eased back into the water to help preserve it as it had begun to break up as it hit the air. The Garda were called. This was now a murder scene and the fire officers began to wonder what terrible chain of events could have unfolded to lead to this poor indi-vidual's severed remains being dumped under Ballybough Bridge. This was beyond anything any of them had encountered before.

The investigation was led by the District Detective Unit and as the area was cordoned off, the news cameras arrived. It was the lead news story and the bulletins were watched in the Mulhall household. After clinging to each other in a fit of tears, Linda and Charlotte made the strange decision to join the crowds gathered near the canal banks to look at the scene themselves. What did they expect to see? Evidence that they were in the clear, or a sure sign that they would be caught?

As well as visiting the crime scene, each replayed their part in the murder over and over in their minds. Marie started to wonder if Charlotte's drunken confession could have had an element of truth to it. Both women looked terrible; a mix of drink, drugs, fear and a lack of sleep was taking its toll.

The killers had had to wrestle with their demons in the days and weeks that followed the discovery of Noor's remains. They had no idea if the investigation would quickly identify Noor or if it would prove impossible. Kathleen pondered the same questions and made a few arrangements of her own. She gradually began to contact Noor's friends to ask about his whereabouts. She said that they'd argued and that he'd moved out. She was looking for him.

Forensic services gave instructions on how best to remove the body parts from the water – a difficult task as the flesh was decaying rapidly and needed to be preserved as best as possible for examination. At this stage, everyone involved assumed the victim was white as the flesh had mottled and bleached. Could it be a gangland killing? Straight away there seemed inconsistencies as a determined criminal could easily scatter the body parts over a wide area, buried in woods and fields, not in a mere six feet of water in a prominent city canal.

The pathologist, Dr Curtis, established that the victim had been stabbed repeatedly but, of course, with the head missing, had no idea of the trauma Noor had received from hammer blows to his skull. Not having a head troubled the team: it would make identification harder. There were items of clothing that had to be removed, socks from the feet and an Irish football shirt plus a pair of underpants. It was when this last item was removed that Dr Curtis noted that the penis of the victim had been severed.

Detectives wondered what nature of crime they were dealing with. There are many ways to dispose of a corpse but dismemberment and genital mutilation pointed to a very disturbed mind. It was a lot to cope with, particularly as small freshwater creatures were exiting some of the wounds. Whoever this man was, he had met a hellish fate.

With genital mutilation came the possibility that the victim may have been part of a 'muti' killing. Four years earlier, a torso of a young boy had been found in the Thames near Tower Bridge in London. No other parts of the corpse had been found. A large-scale investigation covered much of the globe in the Met's efforts to track the identity of the boy they named Adam and find those responsible for his brutal death.

The investigation prompted groundbreaking forensic advances after Detective Inspector Will O'Reilly, the senior investigation officer, asked a group of leading UK scientists for help in establishing where Adam was from. Will O'Reilly had already been advised by experts working on muti crimes in South Africa that the child was unlikely to have been born in Africa. It was based on two facts: first, the boy was uncircumcised, a practice usually carried out shortly after birth in South Africa, and second, his penis had not been removed, a characteristic of muti slayings.

In muti or, to be more exact, its most corrupt practices, the penis is thought to be a source of powerful medicine. The forensic breakthroughs in the Adam case took on two separate strands. First, an advanced use of isotope analysis, in essence, the isotopic signature in food and minerals, means that 'we are what we eat'. This allowed the team to establish that Adam was originally from West Africa, probably from in and around Benin City in Nigeria.

Second, pioneering work found a new route to track a perpetrator using a relative's DNA. This has allowed

UK police to solve other cold cases; although Adam's family and his killers are yet to be identified, it did lead to the exposure of a people-trafficking ring with a direct link to Dublin. When Adam was found, he had been wearing a pair of orange shorts only sold in Germany and it was likely that he was brought from Nigeria, through Germany and then into the UK. Sam Onojhighovie was the link but he went on the run from Germany as the net closed around him, only to emerge in Dublin. He was seeking asylum and, like Noor, claimed to be from a war-torn country, this time Sierra Leone. He was arrested in July 2003 as he was wanted in Germany, where he had been sentenced in his absence to seven years for human trafficking.

The investigation into Noor's murder was led by Detective Inspector Christy Mangan and his team. Like Will O'Reilly, they contacted experts in South Africa to gain their views on whether this murder had the hallmarks of a muti killing. Ultimately, they were advised that it was unlikely that it was, primarily because all organs would have been harvested as part of a ritual killing, not just the penis, and that the victim would have been alive as they were taken. The greater the agony of the victim, the greater the power of the medicine. As Dr Curtis had established that there were no defence injuries on the hands of the victim, it was safe to assume that he had been dead before the dismemberment took place. With an enhanced knowledge of ritual killings, the team now knew that there were fates worse than that faced by their nameless victim.

Dr Curtis had also been able to establish other factors that would help with identification. The victim was black, male and approximately six feet tall. Enquiries were made amongst the black and immigrant communities in the hope that someone would come forward to report a missing friend or member of their family. Quite a few names did arrive at the incident room but all were ruled out.

Posters were produced showing the items of clothing recovered with the body and Linda saw these posters. Her mental health was unravelling and she was experiencing frequent panic attacks. Her next move only added to the sense of disbelief that followed the case some months later. Linda decided to dig up Noor's head.

Why she did this was never particularly clear to the officers involved or indeed Linda herself. She thought it was something to do with wanting to say sorry to Noor. Images of his brutalised body were replayed whenever she closed her eyes and she was paralysed both by a sense of guilt and a gut-wrenching anxiety that she'd be caught, be jailed and lose her children.

She dug up the head, placed it in her son's school bag and walked out into the countryside beyond the nearby village of Brittas. When she arrived at what she thought was a good spot, she sat down and opened the litre of vodka she'd brought with her. She'd also brought a hammer and she attempted to smash the head up into smaller sections to help with reburial. Exhausted and slightly delirious, Linda sat next to the unrecognisable form and started to apologise. She cried bitter tears of regret and pain. No hammer, no vodka and no amount of earth was ever going to hide from herself what she had done.

It took six weeks before the investigation had a breakthrough and it came when Mohammed Ali Abu Bakaar read an article about the torso in the canal and, more importantly, saw the picture of the Irish football shirt that accompanied the piece. He asked around the city chasing up those who might know his old friend but when all admitted that they had not seen him for weeks, he contacted the police.

Bakaar's call was vital, as once the name Farah Swaleh Noor was typed into PULSE, the Garda intelligence database, the team had all they needed to finally establish the victim's identity. Noor's immigration status came up, along with one or two public order offences that he'd been involved in, but there was much more. Noor had been questioned over the murder in 1999 of a seventeen-year-old girl, Raonaid Murray, found dead close to her home in Glenageary, a suburb of Dublin. Also on his file were the contact details of a woman Noor had fathered a child with.

She had contacted the Garda after Noor had made

threats. She reported that he was violent and that it was not the first time that he had threatened to kill her. That information was helping to build a picture of Farah Swaleh Noor's time in Ireland but it was not the crucial piece of the puzzle – it was the son they'd had together who would be able to prove if the torso in the canal belonged to Noor. After a swab from the infant's mouth, tests were carried out and the Garda had their answer – it was Noor.

By tracking Noor's friends and acquaintances, it would be only a matter of time before the gardaí knocked on the door of Kathleen's flat. They arrived on 21 May to what appeared to be a setback – Kathleen had moved out. Yet this helped the investigation as the new tenant allowed the officers in to examine the flat. A section of carpet had been removed, and although the flat looked spotless, it is impossible to eradicate all evidence of blood loss. Specks may not be visible to the human eye but forensic scientists are well-versed in how and where to look. Samples were taken, from surfaces and between cracks in woodwork, and sent for testing. The process is never a speedy one and the results did not come back until late July but when they did, it was what the team needed to hear – the samples were a match for Noor. The team now had enough evidence to make arrests.

DI Mangan's team agreed on how best to approach the four suspects they wished to question: John Mulhall,

Kathleen Mulhall and two of their daughters, Linda and Charlotte. Arrested on 3 August but held for only twelve hours, none of the Mulhalls gave anything away and when they were released without charge, the sisters imagined that the police had run into a dead end. Linda was torn between relief and ongoing attacks of anxiety and nervous exhaustion.

John had watched both daughters as they slid further into alcohol dependency, morbid fear and guilt. His daughter Marie was deeply concerned about her father and the toll it was taking on him. As much as he loved his girls, he could see no other way out than their facing up to the consequences of their still inexplicable actions. He called the police. He wanted to talk.

This was the start of a conversation with John Mulhall that over the next few days and weeks would lead the detectives home to talk to Linda. It would take time, the team walking a tightrope, not wishing to pressure the family but slowly and methodically recruiting their help. Marie also played a key role. She was a voice of reason and told her sisters that what they did would have to be faced. There would be no way out. The police were slowly closing the net and even if they were some way off from a full understanding of what had happened it would only be a matter of time. What was more, it was clear that the mental health of both women was unravelling under the strain.

It was Linda who cracked first. She could not stop

crying but told Mangan all. Over the next few days, Linda gave an account of what had happened that night and it was clear to the experienced detectives in the team that this was no calculated killer, this was a woman barely able to accept what she had done. She tried to show detectives where she had reburied the head but could not find the location. Either scavenging animals had removed it or she was too drunk at the time to recall where she had been.

She was not formally charged until 14 September, the police making sure that her arrest happened after her children had left for school. It was thoughts of her children that haunted Linda most. Imagining life without them left her inconsolable.

Charlotte was not arrested until 17 October, some four weeks after her sister, which was enough time to allow her to lurch from the idea that she was not implicated by Linda to an all-consuming guilt as she knew full well the role she had to play. And now her sister was on remand with four children pining for her.

At first Charlotte tried to suggest that Noor had died before she and Linda got to the flat. Her inventions were never convincing but it was clear that she was bewildered and desperate to see if there was a way she could keep her sister and herself out of jail. Confronted with Linda's final confession, Charlotte eventually broke down and admitted that her sister's account was true.

With both daughters facing a court appearance, Kathleen and John Mulhall reacted in quite unexpected ways. Although both had been questioned and both proved guarded in their answers, the murder had affected the two differently. John, who had nothing but disdain for the man who took his wife from him, found that he could not reconcile himself to what had taken place on 20 March. Shortly before Christmas, he took his own life.

Kathleen, who had always protested that she loved Noor and loved her daughters, sought to save herself. She had proved an adept liar since Noor's murder and with Linda's arrest, fled to Birmingham. She would evade justice for some time, changing her name and her hairstyle on moving to London where she claimed benefits under the name Cathy Ward. She would also become involved with another African immigrant. The mother-of-six was arrested once more in February 2008, and a year later pleaded guilty to clearing up the crime scene where her boyfriend was hacked to death.

In the three years that she was on the run, Kathleen would have heard that her daughters' case had come to trial in Dublin. She would have heard that Charlotte was traumatised by her mother's accounts of Noor's violent episodes and threats. She would have learnt that Linda was genuinely in fear for her safety as the three women were caged in the flat with a volatile Noor, high on alcohol and drugs, and she would have known that her ex-husband took his own life in despair over their actions.

What Kathleen felt when the jury returned its verdict in October 2006 isn't known. The sisters had pleaded not guilty to murder but the jury found 23-year-old Charlotte Mulhall guilty of murder and 31-year-old Linda Mulhall guilty of manslaughter. They returned to court in December for sentencing, Mr Justice Paul Carney commenting that this was one of the most grotesque crimes he had encountered in his professional life. He handed down a life sentence to Charlotte and a fifteen-year term to Linda.

Earlier, Mr Justice Carney had taken a dim view of Linda's defence team when they emphasised that she was a good mother, saying: '...if she was a good mother of four children she would not be getting herself into a situation like that.' In doing so, he echoed the views of many in Ireland who had a degree of sympathy for the women but could never venture to understand the scale of violence unleashed on Noor that night in 2005.

Both defence teams had stressed that the women had come from a tough family background, perhaps in an attempt to explain why a set of disagreements and bad feeling could have spiralled out of all control. But is this reasonable? Marie had grown up in the same environment and yet doggedly stuck to pointing out to her sisters that they had committed a terrible crime and needed to cooperate with the police, as she herself did.

How much are we shaped by our environment? The question continued to arise, particularly when it was learned that, whilst on bail, Charlotte became pregnant and was convicted of prostitution. That left five children facing lives with their mothers behind bars. Kathleen's sons had also been in trouble and two had spoken to the police about their sisters whilst serving time in prison. Were the Mulhalls just one dysfunctional family or were they the symptom of a wider social breakdown in Ireland?

Seeing Charlotte Mulhall holding a knife to the throat of a male inmate inflamed public opinion once more. It was an obscene joke that suggests that Charlotte Mulhall has yet to face up to the full horror of her crime. Linda still grieves over the loss of her children and it is thought that she is struggling to come to terms with how she acted when faced with the threat that Noor posed. She hacked a man to death and dismembered him with brute force. How can her children ever understand that in a loving mother?

She is still haunted by Farah Noor, telling an inmate that she thinks she can now remember where her victim's head was buried. Once she dug it up, she didn't head out into the countryside but came back into the city. She walked to Phoenix Park and after smashing the decomposed skull into smaller fragments, placed the parts in two bags and dumped them in two bins.

If it is true, Noor's head will never be recovered as it

will have been emptied into landfill. Linda may have forgotten but it will not have escaped her attention that Phoenix Park was where John Mulhall chose to hang himself. Was his daughter's confession too much for him to bear?

The sisters and now their mother have many years to find the answers as to what drove them that night in March. Poverty, abuse, drug misuse, alcoholism, depression, fear, anger – perhaps they all have a part to play. But there was something else too. A darkness that gripped the three women, that haunted John and Marie Mulhall, and that troubles all who read of their case still.

CHAPTER EIGHT

Rose Broadley
A Cottage Industry

Unlike all the other stories in this book, this is a tale of a woman who, the courts decided, had not killed.

It is only one who is thoroughly acquainted with the evils of war that can thoroughly understand the profitable way of carrying it on

Sun Tzu

It takes something unusual to cut through the catalogue of drug-related crime in Glasgow and for people to sit up and take notice. They did on a bright spring day at the end of March 2004, and it isn't hard to see why. A presumed drug dealer had been sentenced to life after being found guilty of throwing a prostitute to her death from the twentieth-floor window of a tower block. But this time the killer was a woman.

Rose Broadley looked on impassively as her sentence was read out. Now aged thirty-eight, there was little Rose hadn't seen and little she hadn't ruled out in her gradual and determined effort to shore up her business enterprise. And at first, it seemed that Joanna Colbeck, a 28-year-old working girl and addict, was just an unfortunate casualty of a bad debt. But nothing about this case is as it first seemed and what it reveals is even more terrifying than the news headlines that accompanied Rose Broadley's sentence.

When the police began their investigation into Joanna's death in May 2002, her fear of Rose was openly and widely spoken of. The day before Joanna fell to her death, Rose had dragged her into Robert Butchart's car. Butchart was Rose's right-hand man and once they reached the block of flats where Rose was living, he parked his BMW as Rose gripped Joanna's arm and pulled her into the lift. She beat Joanna, and not for the first time. Although diminutive, Rose was ferocious when crossed and thought nothing of setting about Joanna with her fists, a baseball bat, a length of wood or whatever else was at hand.

Two teenage girls watched Joanna as she was forced into the lift. They saw how terrified the younger woman was. They heard Rose's threats and they did not hesitate to tell the police later what she'd said: 'You wait till you get up the stairs, I have got a surprise for you.

Your name is written all over it'. Joanna was being taken to the twentieth floor, the location of Rose's flat. She will have known what awaited her.

It should never have ended this way. Over the years, Joanna's mother had to watch as her daughter slid into drugs dependency and then took to the streets to raise cash to support her habit. She was just one of over 1,400 women Strathclyde Police estimate are at work at street level at any given time. It is also estimated that as many as 90 per cent of those women and girls are addicts. And the numbers are growing, just as the price of heroin is falling. It is a UK trade now worth a staggering six billion pounds each year but the social and human cost is incalculable.

Janey Godley, an actress and author, wrote in the *Scotsman* about the impact heroin had on the city: 'I lived in the Calton area of Glasgow for 15 years and I saw firsthand what heroin did to a community. The drug flooded the East End of Glasgow, young people were dying and just about every family I knew had an addict. It was shocking. Young girls who were just out of a school uniform were falling out of cars, drugged out of their heads and selling themselves for one more hit. Some of these girls were not even sexually active before they became sex workers.'

Studies in the city have made clear that women working on the streets are engaged in 'survival behaviour' not 'sexual behaviour'. For those who have been mired in poverty, homelessness, abuse – heroin is the perfect trap. Users talk of its ability to flood the body and mind with feelings of warmth and detachment in seconds, providing an intoxicating escape from a grim life and all delivered from a wrap that can cost less than a cappuccino. But users will also admit that they come to choose a hit of heroin over food or paying bills and that, over time, they even choose smack over the needs of their loved ones. This is how the drug debilitates and destroys. The Centre for Drug Misuse Research at Glasgow University found that not only are addict partners failing each other but that 60 per cent of drug addicted parents are failing to provide basic care for their children.

The Centre has provided several studies and evidence to show that some working girls stay on the streets in order to provide for their children but all too often families are destroyed, not sustained, by drug use and prostitution. One working girl poignantly summed up the need to feed her habit by telling the research team of the impact of life on the street. She was asked what had changed as a result of working: 'Ma whole life, everything just everything, ma attitude, I can't get up during the day, I'm not trustful. I'm unreliable. I stole ma brother's watch and I know it's gonna hurt him not because of the fact of the watch but because I'm his sister and I know it'll hurt him but it's me that got to live with it.'

It was a pattern of dependency and abuse Joanna's mother knew all too well. She had endured for years hoping that her daughter would quit the habit – she had heard every promise and she had handed over money time and time again in the belief that things would change. But the change, when it came, was devastating and final.

Rose Broadley was smart. By the time she was of school-leaving age she was a veteran of the rougher parts of Glasgow's Southside. It was clear that she was a woman who should not be crossed. A rumour was that she would pull men in, men like Robert Butchart who'd had their own run-ins with the law, and then manipulate them until they did her bidding. It seemed implausible as Rose hardly looked the femme fatale. She was small, sturdy and every year of her tough life seemed etched on her face. Yet there was something about Rose, something that convinced men that they could be on to a good thing with her, only to find that sooner or later they were marching to her tune.

By her early twenties she was a mum to a boy she called Anthony but the father did not stick around. If she had used heroin, she had insight enough to see that it sucked out the lives of those around her and she changed tack.

The average user is thought to spend around £10,000 a year just to sustain a habit. A spend from users who are predominantly socially marginalised and unem-ployed. They are often homeless too so the question of how to find the thirty pounds or so a day to get by becomes all-consuming. Petty crimes, house break-ins, opportunist thefts and prostitution all spiral in areas where there is a high use of illegal drugs. From time to time, initiatives to get people off the streets and off smack are floated but figures suggest that they are having little or marginal impact. A few will help to break the spiral but they are under-funded, uneven and sometimes short-lived.

Tidying up at the margins is simply not enough to address the root cause of the problem. A long-term and concerted effort is required but it is a thorny political problem. Few politicians are willing to put drugs and prostitution onto the front page without at the same time striking a tough 'law and order' posture. That is hardly surprising as it is estimated that the city's 8,500 heroin injectors commit up to 2.6 million offences a year. The people that they affect most are shop owners and householders – the voting constituency – and people who have suffered may have little time for 'hug a druggie' messages.

Joanna's mother knew first-hand how difficult it was to rehabilitate an addict. Her daughter was caught in a cycle of using that was destroying her. She had run up debts with Rose, as had other girls – the judges at the Court of Appeal said that they 'presumed' these debts to Rose were drug debts. This made good business sense as first, it kept users loyal: if they knew they could 'borrow' an advance, they would do so repeatedly. If a debt accumulated, Rose would take what was owed from their other stream of income: prostitution. It kept customers passive and loyal and all in all it was a sound business model.

Drug dealers are no strangers to marketing. Police officers hear of 'two for one' offers when the market is flooded or the quality of the product dips, they hear of repackaging low quality heroin and rebranding it to keep sales inflated and they've also encountered 'buy heroin, get a crack taster for free'. It is a bleak facsimile of deals on the high street, and all part of the game, where products are shifted and targets met. Markets abhor a vacuum. If a product in demand is illegal there will always be those willing to supply it. It is a wonder that as the great social experiment of Prohibition failed in the 1920s and 1930s in America, we still expect the War on Drugs to end in victory worldwide. Illegal drugs will exist as long as there is a need to escape desperate lives. And drug entrepreneurs were making a profit and all seemed well until May 2000. It was then that the city was hit by a new crisis and at first the police, health officials and even dealers were baffled. It all began in Rose's part of the city – Govanhill.

On the same evening, three women admitted themselves to the Victoria Infirmary in Glasgow. These were no ordinary drug case admissions. The women had abscesses at the point where they injected, in itself not uncommon, but very soon hospital staff were concerned. The women did not respond to antibiotics and their condition deteriorated rapidly. Within hours, they were dead after suffering massive organ failure. This was septicaemia acting at a catastrophic rate and was something staff had not encountered before. It was just the beginning.

Heroin claims one or two lives a week in Glasgow but three fatalities with striking symptoms prompted one of the hospital consultants to call other hospitals to see if this was an isolated event. It wasn't, and over the course of the next few days there were to be nineteen admissions and eight deaths. Seven of the eight deaths were women and it seemed overall that women were being hit the hardest by the flesh-eating bug.

Requests were immediately put out to drug outreach projects warning addicts that if they needed heroin, to smoke and not inject it. Doctors at this stage were unable to pinpoint what was affecting their patients but they knew that each had injected the drug and that all were from the Govanhill area. Why women were being disproportionately affected wasn't clear but project worker Andrew Horne of Turning Point correctly guessed why: skin popping.

Female addicts are far more likely to find it difficult to find a vein to inject into directly and as an alternative they inject directly into their muscle. Whatever was in the bad batch of heroin flowing around the Southside was flourishing inside the muscle, then erupting as abscesses. One female user's abscess grew to twelve inches in diameter and conventional treatments were failing. Doctors had to find out what they were fighting. Samples of the batch were hard to come by and at first the investigation was misled by the fact that thirteen users had used citric acid to break down the heroin for injection, all purchased from the same grocer's shop. Efforts went in to finding out if the citric acid was contaminated but tests produced no link.

It had been declared a health crisis and it was spreading. Clinics as far as Dublin and the north of England found similar cases over the following weeks. Conspiracy theories sprang up amongst users, there was a dealer who hated junkies and was despatching them, the authorities knew but didn't care and so on. In truth, the authorities cared a great deal but it would be another month before health officials got to grips with what they were facing.

Dr Penelope Reading, a consultant microbiologist at the Victoria Infirmary, sent samples of the bacterium for testing, from two users who had survived the outbreak. When the results came back, it was something of a revelation. The bug was clostridium novyi, which can only thrive in the absence of oxygen, often in the bowels. Once inside the body, it can contaminate wounds and cause gas gangrene-like symptoms, last seen in the trenches of World War I. It was not able to establish itself if injected into oxygen-enriched veins, but into the muscle, it was proving deadly.

Dr Reading later admitted: 'We didn't know what organism we were up against, but we knew it was a very aggressive infection that was treated surgically and with antibiotics.' That meant cutting away the infected tissue and hoping that current antibiotics could help the depleted immune system of the addicts fight back. The bug was brutal, causing respiratory as well as organ failure and it would affect 108 users and claim the lives of forty-three people before it ran its course. But what was its source?

There was a rogue batch of heroin. A batch that the police were over 90 per cent certain originated in Afghanistan. As opium is converted to heroin, there was ample opportunity for it to become contaminated with the bug, commonly found in soil and animal remains and able to lie dormant for years. It would also turn out that the initial suspicion that citric acid was responsible did have a role to play in how the bug took hold. The acid is used to break down the consistency of heroin to allow it to be injected but the acid also damages surrounding tissue and this created the right conditions for the spore in the bug to germinate.

The tests also concluded that the contaminated heroin showed evidence that it came from one batch. Proving which batch was a job for the police. Officers had their suspicions and Strathclyde Police chief constable, John Orr, announced that a special unit had been set up to investigate the deaths. He said: 'If someone has supplied such drugs and we can prove it enough to satisfy a criminal court, then that person will be arrested, it's as simple as that.' The crux of the problem was summed up in just six words; 'enough to satisfy a criminal court'. Suspicions and hearsay were plentiful but not evidence. No charges were brought.

The rumours of a dealer with a grudge against users subsided and the streets soon returned to their usual dynamics of supply and demand. It was right that the notion of a vengeful dealer disappeared for one simple reason – dealers don't want to lose customers. If they die because they overdose that's part of the game. But if they die from a contaminated batch, it's bad for business. No dealer would want their pool of users to be depleted. If a link could ever have been established to a single dealer, the police would have found that he or she was a disgruntled one.

Dealers know but do not care that they are dealing

in heroin cut with toxic and dangerous substances –
no heroin goes out 'pure', and users die every week.
They also know that those who manage to stay alive
will lead lives that are destroyed by the drug they
supply and they remain indifferent to that. But the last
thing they will want is their consumers to die en masse.
The distinction may sound trite but it is significant.
And it would prove so on 13 July 2005, the date
of Rose Broadley's appeal for the murder of Joanna
Colbeck.

Rose had been sentenced to life just fifteen months
earlier at the High Court in Glasgow. The police had
compiled a series of statements and evidence that had
convinced the original trial jury, by a majority verdict,
that Rose Broadley had murdered Joanna. There was
footage from CCTV that showed Joanna being manhan-
dled into the lift by Rose, and statements from a man
and his girlfriend who frequently visited Rose's flat in
Norfolk Court. They told the police that they had
witnessed Rose attack Joanna on several occasions.
They painted an appalling picture.

They had watched Joanna being taken into the
kitchen and heard her scream as she was attacked by
Rose, an event they described as Joanna 'getting a
doing'. Another time they found Joanna sitting on the
floor of the flat, crying with a cut to her face. And
there was the time when Rose went 'absolutely
mental', grabbed Joanna by the hair and screamed:

'You fucking cow, I'm going to kill you'. She threatened to stab Joanna and dragged her into a bedroom, kicking and punching her.

In the weeks leading up to her death, Joanna had been hit with a bat and a stick, and in a moment of desperation she said that she would throw herself out of the window. Rose sneered and said: 'Are you going to throw yourself oot the windae? Well, I'll help you!' Tension had risen and not only because of the drug debt Joanna had run up, the girlfriend who'd witnessed the scene said she thought it was exacerbated by the suggestion that there had been 'some sexual activity' between Joanna and Robert Butchart.

The prosecution were able to present evidence of a ten-week period between April and May where Joanna was repeatedly taken off the street, confined in Rose's flat and beaten mercilessly. She was let out only to raise money through prostitution, money which Rose was taking from her. It was a dangerous mix of fury over the unpaid debt and desire to keep Joanna able to turn tricks. And Norman Morton knew Joanna was trapped.

Norman had become involved with Joanna and she would often stay at his flat on the Southside. He wanted to help her but saw that she was helplessly ensnared in her dealings with Rose. He would take his bicycle and ride to meet Joanna at a nearby video shop. He'd persuaded Joanna not to walk the direct route to his home, past a Greggs the baker and a Quicksave shop. This way they were far more likely to elude Rose and Butchart who would cruise the streets looking for Joanna in their BMW. But on the day before Joanna's death, they took the direct route and who should be standing in the bakery but Rose.

Joanna ran. She was running in terror and Norman saw the intent on Rose's face as she pursued Joanna. He heard Joanna scream; she'd run into a dead end and Rose was hitting her. Joanna pleaded for Rose to stop and vowed that her mother would repay the money she owed. Norman saw Butchart and said, 'She's got that lassie petrified, are you going to get her away from her?' Butchart said nothing. Both men watched as Rose pulled Joanna out onto the road and then into the car. Butchart calmly climbed into the driver's seat and drove away.

CCTV footage has become an invaluable tool in police investigations and it was to prove so again in this case. Cameras logged the BMW's arrival at Norfolk Court at 16:05. Rose and Joanna entered the building first, Butchart was logged entering the lift three minutes later. At 17:54 Rose and Butchart were filmed leaving the building and returning at 18:23. During the half hour they were away, the police guessed that Joanna had been left in the flat with Anthony Broadley, Rose's son who was then fifteen.

The next footage would not pick anything up until the following day, 25 May. That afternoon, Tasdaq Shah and Ahsan Ulhaque were in the car park of the mosque not far from Norfolk Court. Looking up, they saw Joanna hanging from a window ledge. They saw her fall. A soundless few moments in time. CCTV footage filmed the moment she hit the ground at 14:09.

The police were called and began to canvass statements. No one answered the door at Rose's flat yet CCTV again caught Rose and Butchart leaving the flats by the back stairs about ninety minutes after Joanna fell. It is quite a walk down from the twentieth floor and the couple were probably attempting to avoid the CCTV in the lift and at the front of the building. It is not clear where the two spent the next few hours but at some point they made the decision to visit Norman Morton. He was woken by them in the early hours of the morning of 26 March and they asked if they could stay. It seems extraordinary that Norman agreed, even after Rose had told him that Joanna had jumped to her death from her flat in Norfolk Court but he may well have felt that he had little choice.

Rose and Butchart stayed in Norman's flat for two days. Norman later told the police that Rose became increasingly agitated. First, she demanded that Norman lie to the police about chasing Joanna and putting her in the BMW. Then an argument flared up about Norman allowing Joanna to wear some of Rose's clothes. It was a confusing rant but Norman remembers being prodded by Rose who made a chilling statement: 'Don't you start me, otherwise you'll be the next to go out the window.'

Rose's son, Anthony, was questioned by the police. He said that Joanna had been staying at the flat and that when he woke up on the afternoon of her death, he noticed that the kitchen window was open. He thought it odd and when he looked out, he saw the ambulance crew and a white sheet on the ground. He checked where Joanna had been sleeping, realised that she was missing and went to wake his mother. After she and Butchart left, he caught up with them and they went to Ibrox where his mother drank heavily. Together they contacted a solicitor and then went to the police to offer their statements.

Suicide was Rose's opinion, Joanna was suicidal. It was a claim Joanna's mother fought vigorously. In her mind, it was clear who was to blame for the death of her daughter. Heroin drove Joanna to the edge but as far as her mother was concerned Rose played a part in her desperate end.

Over the course of the first trial, the majority of the jury believed that Rose had murdered Joanna, but fifteen months later the Court of Appeal took a different view.

First, they emphasised that there was no evidence of fingerprints on the inside window sill, other than Joanna's. The defence argued that no one had seen Joanna being forced out onto the ledge. No one had heard her scream out and when she had been watched from the mosque car park, there was no sign that Joanna had struggled to get back into the kitchen. She simply let go and fell. Suicide was a plausible scenario.

Second, and perhaps more interestingly, they believed Rose would not kill Joanna because she would not wish to dispense with someone who owed her money. The High Court judges, Lords Justices Clerk, Osborne and Johnston, stepped into the mindset of Rose Broadley and made this statement:

'We also consider that it is a legitimate inference to assume that, given the dependence of the deceased on the appellant (Broadley), presumably for drugs and a livelihood and, in any event, owing her money it is more likely than not that she would wish the deceased to remain alive rather than want to kill her.'

So the judges believed that Rose would have kept Joanna alive for commercial reasons. Rose raised a smile when the conclusion was reached: 'In these circumstances, and for these reasons, the appeal is allowed and the conviction for murder will be quashed.' Rose Broadley's conviction for the murder of Joanna Colbeck was overturned.

*

That did not mean that Rose Broadley had been cleared of abduction and assault and she remained behind bars to serve her term for those offences. But she was cleared of murder, much to the dismay of some of the officers who worked on the case.

The decision was reached and has to be abided by yet in one of the areas that the appeal judges highlighted when upholding Rose's appeal, there lies sufficient doubt to cloud the notion that Rose had no part to play in Joanna's demise: the idea that Joanna committed suicide. Both her mother and Norman told the court that Joanna was not suicidal but she was living in fear of Rose. The drugs scene has casualties that roll in off the streets every week. Joanna Colbeck is just one fatality and she will be far from the last.

Hillary Kinnell runs outreach projects for sex workers and has written extensively on the violence working girls face. In her essay 'Murder Made Easy', she analysed the eighty-four homicides of sex workers in the UK between January 1990 and May 2004. She found that although working girls were most at risk from clients, accounting for some 55 per cent of homicides, acquaintances, and specifically drug dealers, were responsible for 17 per cent of prostitute murders. Once drug addiction pulls girls into prostitution, the hazards they face are considerable.

VANESSA HOWARD

Professor Neil McKeganey, from the Centre for Drugs Misuse Research at Glasgow University, doesn't pull any punches. He has seen the impact heroin and other illegal drugs have had on marginalised communities and warns that the problem is snowballing. He was asked what would happen if the problem was allowed to flourish unchecked and said: 'You'd see increasing numbers of children being brought up in homes where there is no structure whatsoever and those children, because they're living with drug-addicted parents, will start to use drugs possibly even at primary school age.'

If they reach school that is. Just before Rose Broadley's appeal was upheld, Mary Pickering was told that she would face a one-year custodial sentence for wilful neglect. The 27-year-old heroin addict was the mother of three-month-old baby girl, Alexandra King, who became infected from her own excrement after she was left in an unchanged nappy and died from septicaemia. The sentence was thought to be light possibly because by the time the trial was under way, Mary was pregnant again.

Perhaps the last word should go to Professor Neil McKeganey, someone who coordinates research coming back from the front line, where the law-abiding see their streets being lost to those making money and those losing their souls in pursuit of the next high. 'This is a problem quite literally tearing the heart out of Scotland,' he said. 'This is the new reality of the "war on drugs", a war that takes casualties like Joanna Colbeck and Alexandra King.'

CHAPTER NINE

Maria Boyne
The Housewife

Three great forces rule the world: stupidity, fear and greed

Albert Einstein

When Maria Boyne gave birth to her third child, staff in the delivery room felt a mix of sorrow and dismay, not because of any complications but because the baby girl had been delivered into a family undone by murder, greed and deception.

Maria was no ordinary mother. There would be no return home for her, flushed with pride, joy and hope for her new daughter's life. She would return to jail and her baby would be taken into care. It is impossible to know what emotions the thirty-year-old felt as she handed over her child – for any other woman, it would have been a moment of unimaginable grief. Yet Maria's story is one of many unimaginable moments, moments that snowballed until the lives of all around her were consumed by her cruelty. On 3 March 2009, Maria Boyne was found guilty of the murder of her husband Graham, but he was not the only one connected to this case to lose his life.

To the casual observer, there was nothing remarkable about Maria and Graham Boyne. They lived on Parkside Avenue in Barnehurst, a commuter town in Bexley that had sprung up in the 1920s. Before the rail link to London, no more than a handful of villagers lived on the Barne estate but by the late 1930s the area had been transformed. Today, it is packed with typical architecture of the period, neat and modest semi-detached homes, with the main focus of the town its railway station and the forty-minute service to Charing Cross.

As a TV repairman, Graham Boyne may not have had the most glamorous of jobs but he was hard-working and was able to provide for Maria and their two young children, a girl of seven and a boy aged five. The Boynes seemed typical of other couples in the area, working to raise a family and getting by as best they could. Behind closed doors, however, the couple were dealing with far more than the usual ups and downs of marriage with two children. Graham was made redundant in 2004 and it hit him very hard. Like many men, he defined himself through his work and a large part of his self-identity was tied up in providing for his family. Later, Graham's mother and father would stress that they had always been proud of their son and that he was conscientious and sociable but they were aware of the pressure he was under after losing his job.

Maria was unhappy. There can be little doubt that a redundancy brings with it more than a loss of income. Graham's self-esteem had taken a hit but Maria found it difficult to lend him any emotional support. Her husband was some eleven years her senior and this was not how she expected married life to be. She expected to be taken care of and could not abide to see Graham slide into what she saw as self-pity. It was a vicious circle. The more that Graham hoped to find comfort and encouragement from Maria, the further she pushed him away. Any doubts he had buried about the long-term prospects for their marriage were brought into painfully sharp relief. It was too much for Graham to cope with and he turned to drinking in the company of friends. It was a safety valve for Graham as he knew more than anyone how damaging the breakdown of a relationship could be and he was desperate to shield his children from the worst.

This wasn't the first time that Graham had been let down by a woman he loved. He knew how it felt to be betrayed, and not just by his lover but by a good friend. He had been married before, again enjoying what seemed to be a conventional marriage, and both he and his wife were outgoing and friendly. He had no idea that over the course of regular nights out, his wife and his best friend had developed an attraction that led to a full-blown affair. When his wife left their home, Graham had to deal not only with the end of a marriage but with the end of a friendship. Perhaps this double betrayal left him not only questioning his judgement but his sense of self-worth; the two people who knew him best had chosen to discard him.

It is not common for men of Graham's generation to unburden themselves on friends. They will provide the bare facts of a situation, admit that their marriage is at an end, for example, but that will be as far as a conversation will go. It is a mix of pride, a need to be seen as emotionally self-sufficient and a desire not to seem weak that means that although they drink, and even drink to excess, they won't necessarily express how they feel. The shutters come down even on those they can trust, such as parents and siblings. Graham's parents guessed how much the loss of a wife and best friend had taken out of their son but they had little idea that there was far worse to come.

When Graham met Maria he felt that maybe his life had taken a turn for the better. Here was an attractive woman over ten years younger who seemed genuinely interested in him. Maria could charm when she wanted to, she was confident and knew how to flirt and Graham seemed like a good prospect. He was solvent, steady and uncomplicated. Perhaps she could find happiness with him, something that had long eluded her.

Something in Maria's past was haunting her, something that led the ordinary fissures in any marriage to rend open, or how else is it possible to explain how she reacted to the breakdown of her relationship? Getting married was not enough, becoming a mother was not enough, there was something pushing Maria to act in an ever more extreme manner.

It started with affairs. Maria may not be the most beautiful woman in the room but she knew how to attract men, mostly by giving out signals that she was sexually available. It did not take long for Graham's friends and family to see this but they were also aware that Graham was desperate for the marriage to work. Maria may not have been able to give him a sense of security but early in their marriage she had given him something he adored – his two children. They were a joy and Graham was very proud of them both; he was a hands-on dad and they responded to his sense of fun and mischief. For Maria, it was different. She had wanted children but found the reality of caring for them more than a burden. She would leave the house and not return for days and even weeks at a time.

Whilst she was away, Graham would hear reports that she had been seen with other men, men he knew she was probably sleeping with. Graham's dependency on alcohol worsened as his marriage fell apart. He found it hardest not that his wife was sleeping around but that she would stay away from their home for so long that she even missed the children's birthdays. This was unforgivable. Whatever difficulties they faced as a couple, Graham was determined that the children should not be exposed to it. Despite his reliance on alcohol, he managed to keep the household running and the children felt safe in his care. Yet something had to give.

At first, it seemed hopeful. By late 2007, Maria decided that she would try again to make the marriage work and Graham was delighted. Family members had their reservations but knew that Graham wanted the best for the children and they were left to hope that the couple could find a way to work out their differences. In reality, all the warning signs were there. Maria was unable to commit to Graham or the children and had repeatedly indulged in destructive behaviour. To be dissatisfied with a marriage is one thing but to repeatedly leave the marital home for weeks at a time smacks of abusive disregard for others. The children were robbed of any sense of security from their mother, she clearly placed her impulses before their welfare and they were left bereft at each abandonment.

Something drove Maria to find affirmation outside the home. Men she could attract, diversions that kept her amused, anything but face up to her responsibilities. Yet she could not make a clean break. If this suggested a prick of consciousness, her later actions would expose it as little more than self-interest. Starkly put, Maria had nowhere else to go. She needed a roof over her head and Graham still provided that.

And so the stage was set. Graham had suffered setbacks both when his first wife left him and when he was made redundant, leaving him emotionally vulnerable. Maria did not support him as a spouse should, yet he found that he could not end their relationship. In part this was because of his worries for his children but it is possible that subconsciously, in winning her approval, he felt that he could recover from his previous losses. His sense of well-being was distorted by a dependence on Maria; the more she humiliated him, the more he was pulled into wanting her. The stakes grew ever higher.

Maria was also addicted to the dynamics of their relationship. She enjoyed humiliating Graham and every time he forgave her, it fuelled her disregard. In essence, anyone who saw her worth was fit to be despised. It is highly likely that this was a situation played out in her early childhood. It is not uncommon for girls that grow up in dysfunctional and volatile environments to find themselves repeating the pattern in their adult relationships.

Chasing men was one aspect of a need for approval, neglecting children another. Many emotionally and physically abused children talk about the difficulties in forging bonds once they reach adulthood. Seeing a needy child, or partner, reminds them of their child-hood, a time when their needs were not met and they were subject to cruelty. Sometimes these women turn their role as a child victim into one where she is the aggressor, the one in control as an adult.

Maria had an emotional hold over Graham and a key role in providing stability in her children's lives but she consistently let them down. Despite announcing that she would return to Graham late in 2007, it was not because she had chosen to start afresh, it was no more than the next step towards a bloody end.

It was difficult to watch from the outside of the marriage and remain neutral. Graham's parents, Michael and Joan, lent what support they could but had to accept that their son did not want the marriage to end. They had to focus on the positive, the fact that their two young grandchildren would have both parents home for Christmas.

Although Michael could not influence Graham's belief that Maria would change her ways, he was deter-mined to help his son battle his addiction to alcohol. As a retired ambulance man, Michael had seen what alcohol could do to a man. All too often, ambulance medics are on the front line when it comes to dealing with drunk and disorderly behaviour. Numbers have spiralled over the last decade with the London Ambulance Service alone attending over 61,000 alcohol-related incidents in a one-year period. The last decade has seen deaths from alcohol abuse soar and hospital admissions stand at over 207,800 per year from injuries, assaults, liver cirrhosis and alcohol-related heart disease.

It is a grim set of statistics but the numbers cannot measure the emotional toll that it places on the loved ones who live with, or care for, the alcohol dependent. It is a daunting task to persuade someone you love to find the strength to resist self-harming but Graham's parents and sister Elaine were determined to help. It would be Michael who would finally convince his son that he needed to accept that his drinking was a problem and together they sought help. Alcohol Dependency Units provide counselling and help users understand why and how they came to misuse alcohol, often the key to breaking the addiction.

This was a step in the right direction as alcoholism would have been detrimental to Graham's mental and physical health over the long-term and he was determined not to disappoint his son and daughter. With Maria back at home, he felt that his life could get back on track. It wasn't to be. Maria met Gary.

Gary McGinley lived on Franklin Road, some two miles from Graham and Maria's Parkside Avenue home. He was a warehouseman and only 23 years old when he met Maria. Gary was sociable but somewhat naïve and had learning difficulties. Despite being back in the family home with the understanding that it was to repair her marriage, Maria embarked on an affair.

Gary was quite different from Graham. First, there was the age gap, Gary was six years younger than Maria who was by then nearing thirty. It probably reflected a different dynamic to Maria, who found the young man easy to manipulate as he was soon besotted with her and she began to plan a future with him. This was a departure from her other relationships. Other men had come and gone, some perhaps sensing that Maria Boyne was potentially a dangerous woman, others she simply cast off once the first flush of an illicit affair lost its appeal.

The reality of her situation began to plague Maria. She was not a free agent, she was a married mother of two and that could not be simply erased in favour of some new romance. She decided she was in love with Gary, she wanted a wholly new life but felt constrained by her past. Other women in a similar situation, where a marriage had run its course, would simply pick up the phone and contact a family lawyer to ask for advice. But not Maria. In her mind, new and dangerous fantasies began to take hold.

She told a friend and neighbour about her unhappiness and began to sound more and more infuriated by Graham's legitimate claim to the home. What began as a rational assessment that the house 'was half hers' started to veer into claims that would disturb her friend. This friend would later tell the police that Maria had said: 'If Graham wasn't here, I'd have my own house back.'

The idea that Maria somehow 'owned' the family home started to take a sinister turn. With ownership came the sense of entitlement and any dissatisfaction she felt about Graham's failures as a husband snowballed into toxic hostility.

Her reasoning was perverse. Graham had been the breadwinner and the only anchor the children had known. Maria had not contributed to the upkeep of the home and had proved an upsetting and disruptive presence in her children's short lives yet she had convinced herself, in the full throes of a new affair, that the block to her happiness and security was Graham. She openly spoke of her frustration to a neighbour and said that she had considered putting sleeping pills in her husband's vodka, to 'rid herself of Graham for once and for all'. This was more than bravado, this was a mind contemplating murder.

It is an almost impossible step for a balanced mind to take. We have all experienced anger but very, very few will allow that rage to push them to take someone's life. It is possible to imagine striking out in self-defence or to sense that we would use any means necessary to protect a loved one and yet what Maria was mulling over was to kill a man she had once loved, the man who was the father of her children.

The criminal justice system is designed to assess every shade of human motivation and error, from accidental fatalities to premeditated murder. The police are tasked with gathering evidence, evidence that will be presented before the court and used as a basis for the jury to arrive at a verdict of guilt or innocence. Juries are sophisticated enough to understand differences even if the scenario and outcome are the same.

For example, a man has been charged with murder after he went out drinking, pushed a man over and it resulted in a fatal head injury. If the accused had been seen acting aggressively throughout the night, harassing passers-by and shoved one of them into the road, then a verdict of manslaughter would be reasonable. If, however, the intoxicated man broke up a fight and one of the men he'd separated reached for a knife and lunged towards him, pushing the man away in self-defence would be viewed differently.

We each have the capacity to imagine placing ourselves in different scenarios and know what 'reasonable force' means in each, which is why the term is so loosely defined. We are all sophisticated enough to understand the drives and impulses of others, we know that some relationships break down and the unhappiness that can cause and, in the main, we are reluctant to condemn those caught up in the end of a marriage, but we are also aware that the option to walk away is always open to women like Maria.

Was she so cut adrift from reality then, that she imagined that her neighbour would be sympathetic towards her plans to 'rid' herself of Graham? Did she imagine that she could then act out her murderous fantasies and that her neighbour would remain silent? And did she think that her affair with Gary would go unnoticed? In the months and weeks that led up to Graham's death, Maria made every mistake possible as if she believed she could get away with murder.

This was more than poor judgement, Maria was drifting into an arena where no one could challenge her twisted thinking. Certainly not Graham, who was still hoping for a reconciliation, and not Gary who was too slow to realise what kind of woman he was entangled with. Maria was no longer interested in right and wrong, she was only interested in playing out a fantasy whereby her past was jettisoned and Gary sat in Graham's place. By the start of 2008, there was a new impetus to her thinking: Maria was pregnant.

Again, she had every opportunity to simply break the news to her long-suffering husband and walk away. Yet her interest in ridding herself of Graham and replacing him with Gary only grew. How much Gary knew of his girlfriend's plans is not clear, even today. What the police were able to uncover, however, were the most brazen acts of deceit and betrayal.

Maria booked into the Dartford Holiday Inn with Gary. That Wednesday evening, her children were not at home but she knew that Graham was. The last person who saw him was his father, Michael. He called in on the evening of 23 April at around six p.m. They had arranged to attend an alcohol addiction clinic the following morning and after a quick chat, Michael left.

It was late in the evening. Maria left the Holiday Inn and Gary drove her the few miles to Parkside Avenue where she knew that Graham was waiting. She had made the suggestion that if they were to start rebuilding their marriage fully, they should spend the night together. Maria knew that alcohol was an addiction for him yet she talked Graham into drinking with her that evening. She then persuaded him to go upstairs to the bedroom, to undress and wait for her.

Graham did as she asked. He had no idea of what would happen over the next few minutes and in truth he never had a true idea of what his wife was capable of. Maria entered the bedroom with two knives behind her back. Graham was lying face down as Maria raised her arm above her head and struck him. She attacked him with single-minded ferocity, raining twenty-two blows onto his back and five into his torso as he twisted and tried to resist his wife's attack.

He did not stand a chance. Despite his strength, he was weakened from alcohol, blood loss and shock. He fell back onto the bed and Maria stood over him as his life slipped away. Now she had to think. Her first thought exposed her venality to the full. She looked down at Graham's gold necklace, wiped off the blood and wondered how much she could get for it.

How did she imagine that she could get away with

cold-blooded murder? Standing in the bedroom she had shared with her husband, her first thought had been to make some quick cash from pawning Graham's necklace, the second was to recruit Gary in creating the flimsiest of stories as to what happened to Graham.

Where was Gary? The police were meticulous in their efforts to build a picture of the couple's movement on the night but admit that there are gaps when either of the two are not picked up in witness statements or on CCTV. But one neighbour told the police that she saw Gary McGinley standing opposite the house at around eleven thirty p.m. Was he waiting for Maria to finish her work?

The police were able to establish that Maria had no credit left on her mobile phone. This would not stop her receiving calls but when they traced the messages left on Gary's phone, another possibility came to light. A call was made from the BT phone box closest to Parkside Avenue at 1.01 a.m. A message was left on Gary's mobile phone. It said: 'Have you got a problem? I need to know.' The voice was male. Had Gary given Maria his phone? Was the voice Gary's, checking that all had gone to plan?

At that moment, there was a problem and Maria was determined to enlist Gary to help solve it.

Gary would later tell the police that he arrived at the house on Parkside Avenue to pick Maria up but he did not think that she had carried out her threat to harm her husband. He said: 'Maria was upset and crying. She said she killed Graham. I didn't believe her at first, then I saw blood on her hands. I went into the house and she was screaming, "What have I done?"'

If Maria was hysterical, it was a moment that passed as no neighbour reported hearing her wails of anguish. Gary went upstairs and saw Graham lying on the blood-soaked bed. He told the police that Maria had told him that she had killed him so that they could be together. It made him feel guilty, he said, particularly as Maria stressed that as she was carrying his child, he should do all he could to help her. Neither of them helped Graham, however. Gary suggested calling an ambulance but said that Maria overruled him. She showed no mercy.

They left the house, with the necklace, and set off for Southend. There was a key sighting of Maria at six fifteen a.m. A neighbour saw Maria walking out of the house alone. If Graham had been killed hours earlier, what was she doing at the property? Was this a sighting of her after she returned to pick up some items, perhaps even looking for more things to use to finance her trip to Southend? Maria has yet to provide any explanation as she sees little to be gained by telling the truth.

Before they reached Southend, the couple drove to the Morrisons supermarket in the nearby town of Erith, which is set on the Thames. Maria later claimed that Gary told her to throw one of the knives into the river and she walked along the pier to do just that. Why the other knife wasn't also thrown away isn't clear. After Gary's car was searched, a knife with an ornamental handle was found in the boot but forensics were unable to establish if it was the knife used to kill Graham.

Once they reached Southend they set about finding a bed and breakfast to book in for the evening. They then found a pawn shop in the town and cashed in Graham's necklace for £220. Some of the money would be used to pay for the guesthouse they were staying in and some was spent on shopping. As a token of her affection, Maria handed what was left of the money to Gary as a gift. The proprietor noticed that the couple seemed carefree, were laughing and sharing jokes.

Some ninety miles away, back in Barnehurst, Graham's father could not understand why his son was not ready and waiting for him. He entered the house and called out. Then he walked upstairs and into his son's bedroom and life as he knew it ceased. The scene was brutal – he tried to register and process all that was before him and tried to use his skills as a paramedic to help Graham but it was too late. His son had lost his fight for life hours earlier in the bleak and dark early hours of that April morning.

Everyone wondered where Maria was. The police tried to contact her immediately, as the next of kin, but she was nowhere to be found. It was then that a neighbour told the police that they had seen Maria at around six fifteen a.m. But how was that possible? That was some three hours before the body of her husband was discovered. The police knew that there were more questions than answers at the crime scene and that locating Maria was a priority.

Maria was doing some thinking of her own. She knew that she could not evade being spoken to about the events at her family home and so she devised a story that she hoped would put her in the clear. She asked Gary to drive her back to Barnehurst, imagining that the trip would help provide her with an alibi for her movements. She called Graham's parents but could not get an answer. It is difficult to imagine what she would have said to them had they had been home, perhaps they were to be a sounding board for her narrative.

Next she called her sister who broke the terrible news. 'I know,' Maria said when told that her husband was dead. Of course she knew but it is clear that any attempt to feign ignorance had been shelved.

Her sister advised Maria to contact the police. Maria decided she was ready and walked into a local station at Bexleyheath. Gary would not come forward for another two days.

Maria wanted the local CID to understand that she had nothing to do with her husband's death. But Maria would not be dealing with the local unit alone. An incident room had been set up in Lewisham and Detective

Inspector Graeme Gwyn of the Met's Homicide and Serious Crime Command would lead the enquiry.

Maria was interviewed and the police began carefully to piece together all that had happened in the early hours of 24 April. Police interviews bear little resemblance to those featured on TV and in films. The settings are similar in that they depict nondescript rooms with a tape recorder and two detectives, and sometimes a legal representative, present. But the manner in which detectives approach interviews is a world away from the fraught and confrontational showdowns that are seen on screen. It is not an interrogation and detectives are trained not to intimidate those they interview.

The person interviewed is made aware why they are being questioned, they are repeatedly advised of their rights, asked if they want legal counsel present, asked if they would like a break and in all ways encouraged to take ownership of proceedings. Detectives do not ask hostile or difficult questions, they emphasise that they are only gathering responses to their questions.

To an outsider, the structure of interviews seems oddly low key and painstakingly polite but it is for good reason. Detectives have to ensure that the statements they gather will hold up under rigorous examination by a defence barrister. If there is any suggestion that the statement was given under duress or if the defendant was ignorant of their rights, the whole case could collapse.

This softly softly approach can also pay dividends as some of those questioned find they can spin explanations for their movements at the time of the crime without being challenged. Detectives will not argue with those they question and say, 'that sounds like a lie' or 'that is hardly the action of an innocent person', they will simply collate what has been said and then slowly focus on any inconsistencies. There will have been quite a few to draw Maria Boyne's attention to.

Maria stated that she had been at home with Graham when an intruder came into the family home. A man she described as having 'wild staring eyes'. Graham challenged the intruder and Maria was too afraid to intervene. It was quite an elaborate fiction that deliberately left out any mention of Gary McGinley. Her story was carefully noted in full and then one of the detectives asked why, with an intruder in the home, had Maria not called the police? Maria had also stated that Graham had been injured as he grappled with the intruder and so the question was put, why had Maria not called for an ambulance? She had no plausible answer to give to either question.

The home on Parkside Avenue had been cordoned off and a search of the property and surrounding drains had failed to uncover the murder weapons. Statements from friends and relatives were taken and slowly a picture of the couple's life was put together. Phone records were examined too and it was clear that calls

VANESSA HOWARD

had been made on the evening of Graham's death –
two-way traffic between Maria Boyne and Gary McGinley.

Gary was questioned too and the police felt sufficiently confident to charge both with the murder of
Graham Boyne. They appeared before Bexley Magistrates Court on 28 April, just five days after the discovery of Graham's body. For a woman who had long been
obsessed with the family home, the police press release
was a stark reminder of the reality of the life she had
chosen – Maria was described as unemployed and of
no fixed address.

Maria and Gary were held on remand until their trial
could begin at the Old Bailey almost a year later in
February 2009. It was a long time to be held, long
enough for Maria to give birth to her third child and
long enough for her to think about the statement she
had made to the police.

She knew by then that Gary had told the police of
their affair, the fact that they had stayed at the Holiday Inn and had sex before she left to travel to Parkside Avenue and meet Graham; he told them about the
phone calls and that by the time he'd arrived at the
house, Maria admitted that she'd killed her husband.
What could she do, now that Gary had left her with
all the blame? She was not going to be left high and
dry, not by Gary McGinley, not by any man.

Following Gary's sudden admission early in the trial

226

that Maria had thrown one of the knives into the Thames at Erith, the police Marine Search Unit had combed the riverbed in the hope of finding the weapon. At first it seemed like a hopeless task but after wading in viscous mudflats for two days, the knife was found lodged near the pier. Maria was shown a picture of the knife. She said it could have been the murder weapon.

By the time the trial began, the Boyne family were still struggling to come to terms with their loss. Graham's father Michael said: 'The shock of finding my son in this manner has affected me deeply. I cannot sleep at night; thoughts keep going through my head.' The impact on Graham's two children had been equally devastating. Michael said that his eight-year-old grand-daughter had run around her former home, looking for her father, and was inconsolable. He added: 'She said she wanted to die so she could be with her daddy.' His six-year-old grandson asked when his daddy would come back.

It isn't known if Maria spent time thinking about what she had brought to the lives of her two eldest children. Her decision to 'rid' herself of Graham had effectively left them orphaned. Michael Boyne said: 'We had to find a lot of courage within ourselves to tell the children their father had been killed and their mummy was in prison with Gary, having been accused of killing him.' Two young children faced a life of emotional turmoil knowing that both parents were lost to them through one savage act of selfishness. One further child, still an infant, would grow up to learn that her parents had both been accused of murder.

The question for the jury would be to determine who was guilty of Graham's murder – Maria, Gary or did they act as accomplices? The trial would be further complicated by Maria's sudden decision to retract the statement she gave to the police and to tell them that the killer was known to her. The man responsible for the murder was Gary McGinley.

Maria said that she had lied only to try and protect her lover, the father of her then unborn child. It had been Gary's idea to rid themselves of Graham and he had called her when she was at home and in bed with her husband. After the second call, in the early hours of the morning, she decided to get dressed, to go down-stairs to use her mobile phone and ask Gary what he wanted. He told her he was outside waiting and to open the door.

Maria let him in. Gary entered the hallway and she saw that he had a knife tucked into his waistband – a large carving knife in a black leather case. She asked him what he was doing and he told her: 'You know why I am doing this.' He then motioned for her to be quiet and began to walk up the stairs.

Maria claimed: 'It did not cross my mind that he would use the knife' but that she then heard Graham cry out, 'Help me!' In a panic, Maria ran into the street but Gary followed her and stopped her from contacting the police. She listened to him because she loved him and she was carrying his child. They then drove to Gary's flat where he changed his clothes and they then decided to return to the house in Parkside Avenue. It was then that they took Gary's necklace and cleaned the blood from it, before setting off to Southend.

The jury were left to assess two differing accounts of the events and they spent hours sifting through all the evidence that had been presented to them. The first verdict was reached on 27 February after twenty-three hours of deliberation. The foreman informed the judge that they found the defendant guilty of the charge of murder. Maria Boyne listened impassively and wondered what would be Gary McGinley's fate. Three days later, he was acquitted.

Judge Paul Worsley told Maria Boyne that she would have to serve at least twenty-four years in prison before being considered for parole. DI Gwyn gave his assessment of Maria Boyne's character saying: 'Throughout the investigation and trial Maria Boyne constructed a self-serving and complex web of deceit, which the jury were able to see through in reaching their verdict.'

Justice was seen to be done but it would afford little comfort to the Boyne family as Maria's cruel act had claimed another victim. Michael Boyne had not been in court to hear the verdicts. On 23 February, he told his family to attend the court session without him as he felt too unwell to travel with them. When they arrived home that evening, they found that Michael had collapsed. He died the following day in hospital. In less than a year, Joan Boyne had lost a son and her husband.

Michael had done all he could for his son, he knew of his battle with alcohol addiction and was determined to help him, he knew how much his marriage troubled him but was on hand to lend advice and support whenever he could. It was no more than any parent would do and yet his actions, and those of his wife and daughter, were a world away from the calculating and destructive impulses Maria Boyne allowed to sway her. She thought nothing of her son and daughter, nothing of the man she had once loved and nothing of the family who had always stood by them. She thought only of herself and her latest affair.

Judge Paul Worsely said: 'You left Graham's father to discover the bloodied corpse of his son. That was unforgivable … This was a murder with a view to gain. You had repeatedly told others that you had intended to get your hands on the house and do whatever it took to achieve that aim. You were also motivated by sex and selfishness.'

It is impossible to know how much of the judge's statement Maria took in as she remained expressionless throughout the session. The newspapers would pick up on the story and much was made of Maria's determination to kill for right to inherit 'the £150,000 home'. Maria denied that this was her motivation and the only hint as to her true state of mind on the night of the murder was that she had experienced an 'emotional firestorm' at the time of the killing.

It is an insight that should not be entirely dismissed. However much she planned and visualised Graham's death, it would have borne little resemblance to the night itself. To pick up two knives and attack another human being as Maria did requires a state of frenzy. Graham did try to defend himself and yet her wrath was sufficient to overpower him, someone who was stronger and taller. She did not kill him through lashing out with one blow. This was a cataclysmic and sustained rage.

Perhaps Maria is yet to come to terms with what drove her to such a brutal act, perhaps she is yet to reconcile the events in her past with the extreme violence she used that evening in April. Something had always pursued Maria. It drove her away from a caring and decent man who gave her a home and offered her forgiveness, it drove her away from two young children who needed and deserved a caring mother and it drove her to the ultimate betrayal. Not an affair or pregnancy by another man but luring someone who loved her into the bedroom when she knew he would never be able to hold his children again.

VANESSA HOWARD

This was a terrible and selfish act and yet it served no one. Maria does not have the home, she does not have Gary and she does not have her children. She has the blood of one man on her hands and it can be argued that the grief she caused contributed to the untimely death of his father. Maria was looking for a home. It is hard to believe now that she will ever find one.

CHAPTER TEN

Tracey Connelly – Mother of Baby P
'I failed my son'

Thou art thy mother's glass
William Shakespeare

The infant was dead before help could reach him. Fractured ribs, a broken arm, a face disfigured with bruising; the boy lay in a blood-stained cot long after life had ebbed away. His mother and her boyfriend were only dimly aware that this time the boy would not wake up, this time they had gone too far. The boyfriend, a man who had sexually assaulted another child, told his girlfriend to dial 999 and say that her son had stopped breathing.

The facts seem familiar and yet they are not those that belong to the last day of Peter Connelly's life, the toddler known to us at first as Baby P. This was another boy, two-month-old Rhys Biggs, who died in May 2006 after a number of horrific assaults and a year before Peter was killed in a home only ten miles away in east London. Rhys's mother, 27-year-old Claire Biggs, was found guilty of 'wilful assault' and her boyfriend, 33-year-old Paul Husband, guilty of 'wilful neglect'. Claire Biggs had another child, already on the 'at risk' register but no background checks had been run on Husband, who had previously sexually assaulted a seven-year-old girl, because the nature of their relationship was 'unclear'.

Again, the parallels with Peter's case are depressingly similar and the NSPCC caution that no matter what the outcry, these two cases will not be the last. In fact, even as the tabloid headlines ran and questions were asked in parliament, children were dying in the care of their mothers. From the day Peter was found dead in his sparse and filthy room on 3 August 2007 to the time his mother faced trial in November 2008, it is estimated that another forty-five children aged under five were murdered by those charged with caring for them. Children are brutalised and killed with shocking regularity in the UK yet there was something about Baby P that convulsed the nation. Why this case, more than any other case?

In was in November 2008 that the public learnt that Peter had been found dead with a horrific catalogue of injuries. His spine had been snapped in two, possibly over the knee of one of his tormentors or perhaps by being smashed over a banister. His ribs were fractured, some fingernails were missing, possibly ripped out, his head shorn and scarred, his face a mass of bruising. It would take a post-mortem to learn that one of his milk teeth had been punched out so violently that Peter had swallowed it.

Sometimes, when cruelty is on a scale that is impossible to comprehend, it is the small detail that breaks the heart. All parents know what a milestone it is to see a baby smile and proudly show his first tooth. Milk teeth are often kept long after the child reaches adulthood, as are locks of hair after a baby's first haircut. They are mementos, stepping stones in a happy childhood that parents cherish. But not all parents. And that lies at the heart of our outrage.

Much of the disgust the public felt was directed at the social and health care workers involved in the case. The press highlighted the fact that Peter was seen on sixty occasions and yet he was still returned to his mother's arms. It seemed incredible: how could the eyes of the state remain so blinkered as a baby suffered so severely? The cruellest moment seemed to be when Peter was examined by Dr Sabah al-Zayyat, a locum paediatrician at St Ann's Hospital. She failed to examine the 'cranky' baby fully – at this stage, Peter had shattered ribs and probably a severed spine. She noted bruising to his face and back, a infection in his ear and a fungal infection on his scalp and sent him home with anti-biotics. Within forty-eight hours, he was dead.

The furore reached government at the highest level and it led to senior figures at Haringey Social Services losing their jobs: Sharon Shoesmith, head of children's services, was sacked. Council leader George Meehan, and Liz Santry, the cabinet member for children and young people, resigned. Their roles were to manage the strategic direction of childcare services in the borough and they were seen to have failed.

More sackings were to follow, this time amongst the ranks of social workers responsible for safeguarding children on a day-to-day basis: Clive Preece, Maria Ward, Gillie Christou and Cecilia Hitchen. Maria Ward was appointed as Peter's caseworker six months before his death and she had visited Peter's home several times. If public anger was assuaged to some extent by removing social workers from their posts, the harder truths of this case are still to be faced. Whilst social services may have failed seventeen-month-old Peter, it was neglect of a more pernicious kind that led to his death – how could a mother stand by and let her baby be tortured and killed?

The public were not given a name for Peter's mother, or at least not through legal means at first. The name Peter was released but not his last name, the names of his siblings, the boyfriend, the lodger or his mother. They were kept out of the press, in part to protect the identity of Peter's siblings but also because another case was pending. In May 2009, the mother's boyfriend, already one of the three found guilty of causing Peter's death, was found guilty of raping a two-year-old girl in the home where Peter died.

The names of Peter's mother and her boyfriend were leaked onto internet chat rooms, however, and even their addresses featured alongside a group that expressed the desire for violent retribution. Its title is revealing; it was called: 'Death is too good for Tracey Connelly, torture the bitch that killed Baby P.' If this was mob-vigilantism, it revealed a genuine revulsion and the notion that if the mother were to experience some of the pain inflicted on her helpless son, that would be a just reward for her neglect. The anger was palpable and it was driven by the fact that this case touches on a taboo – mother as abuser. Far beyond case-workers and even beyond the anger felt towards the boyfriend, it was Peter's mother who became the figure of hate and blame.

As a society we idealise the role of motherhood, believing that women are naturally caring and nurturing. Anna Motz is a clinical and forensic psychologist who works with female offenders and has seen how sentimental attitudes towards motherhood cloud judgement, often with disastrous results. In her book *The Psychology of Female Violence*, she writes: 'I consider this to be a fundamentally dangerous social attitude, which can lead to vilification of those who do display violence to the extent that they are considered inhuman and "evil", and, at the other extreme a massive denial of risk to children who may remain under the unsupervised care of abusive mothers and carers.'

It is an astute summary on two counts. First, we do recoil in horror when we hear that a mother is violent, or allows violent treatment, towards her children as subconsciously we believe that is somehow to be expected of men, but not women. In truth, statistical evidence makes for uncomfortable reading. Whilst, on average, men are responsible for 87 per cent of all homicides and serious violent crimes, it is women that account for over 65 per cent of infanticides. Women are a consistent risk when it comes to their children and yet when a shocking case hits the headlines, questions of why get lost in a blizzard of outrage. We need more than outrage to protect children.

Second, Motz makes the point that our latent belief that 'mother knows best' can leave a child at risk longer than it is rationally justifiable. How else is it possible to explain why Peter, and others like him, are left in the care of an inadequate mother? Despite the dog mess, dead mice, human faeces, pornographic magazines and even a dismembered rabbit scattered in the squalor of the home, social workers believed that Peter's needs would be best met in his mother's care.

The legislation underpinning social services for children and young people is based on the Children Act 1989. Within it, local authorities are advised that: 'Provided that this is consistent with the child's safety and welfare, to promote the upbringing of such children by their families, by providing services appropriate to the child's needs.' The key guideline here is that children should remain with their families, and in the overwhelming majority of cases that will mean the mother. The consensus for some time has been that a child will fare best if cared for by its mother and whilst there is research to back up the rather obvious point that if the mother has sound parenting skills, that is the case, it can be argued that there is a 'blind spot' when it comes to assessing a mother's abilities. Biology is not enough.

As a species, we are programmed to reproduce and to ensure that our offspring thrive – but not always. Human history catalogues the death of infants: sometimes infanticide was used as a form of population control, at other times used to eradicate 'defects' in newborns. Academic researchers have noted another aspect of infanticide. In their book *Endangered Children*, Lita Schwartz and Natalie Isser found: 'that statistically infants ... are 60 to 70 times more likely to die at the hands of a stepparent than a natural parent, confirming evolutionary biologic analysis that stepparent homicide is the pattern observed in other creatures such as insects, birds, primates, and other mammals'.

Clearly, the instincts surrounding parenting are more complex than we first imagine and an investigation of the motivation underpinning infanticide also needs to take into account perhaps the most significant factor of all – the mental health of the mother. British law pioneered the idea that motherhood could mentally destabilise a woman and the Infanticide Act of 1922 provided a defence for women who had killed their newborns. As the death penalty was still in existence, the Infanticide Act accepted temporary insanity as a mitigating factor and in doing so, capital punishment did not have to be imposed. Post-partum psychosis is a recognised condition but is very rare, affecting less than 0.2 per cent of new mothers. It is an extreme condition, striking in the first days and weeks of motherhood and is a form of acute psychosis. The mother may experience hallucinations, hear voices and suffer debilitating anxiety attacks and may try to harm her baby – it is not to be confused with the far more common condition of post-natal depression.

When two-year-old Romario Mullings and his three-month-old brother Delayno were found stabbed to death, their mother, 21-year-old Jael Mullings had reached the end of a long and desperate struggle. As well as calling her GP, Mullings had previously left Romario in A&E in a hospital in Manchester and a few months later, left him at a doctor's surgery. Both boys were known to social services but as Mullings's mind unravelled further in 2008, no one stepped in and removed her sons from her care. Suffering with paranoid schizophrenia, Mullings has been detained indefinitely in a secure psychiatric hospital. She is said to have shouted out: 'I'm a child of Israel. I'm a mother and brought life into the world. I'm also the devil so I can take life away.' Hers was a tragic but very rare case.

All these steps lead us closer to understanding where the real danger lies for babies such as Peter, Rhys Biggs and the nameless others who are not even on the radar of overstretched social workers, because psychosis is rarely what lies behind neglect and abuse. Tracey Connelly was not schizophrenic and as details about life in her Tottenham home emerged, anger grew. If a mother is mentally ill, the public has a degree of sympathy but when it was alleged that Tracey spent her days chatting online, visiting poker sites, drinking and watching porn, any attempt to build an understanding vanished.

Although it became clear that Peter's main tormentor was Tracey's boyfriend, later named as Steven Barker, fury towards the mother did not wane. It may have been Barker who used the pliers on the defenceless toddler, it may have been his dog that terrorised the child, it may have been Barker that threw the boy 'like a rag doll' but as it became clear that Tracey did nothing to intervene, incredulity hardened to revulsion.

In the eyes of the law, not taking part in the physical torture of Peter was no defence, and rightly so. The

VANESSA HOWARD

impact of neglect on a child is devastating and is in itself a form of aggression. The woman who starves her child of comfort can damage a child more than the mother who lashes out at her child in a moment of anger.

In the last few months of his brief life, Peter was seen to shovel soil into his mouth in his back garden, he cried continually as he remained wearing unchanged filthy nappies that led to ulcerated rashes, his face was swollen with bruising and his scalp infected with sores. She saw all this, his mother. Tracey Connelly did nothing.

Yet it was worse than a failure to intervene, to save her defenceless infant – Tracey elected to cover up the abuse of her son. There has been a good deal of speculation that Barker intimidated the household, that his compulsive violence led to an air of dominance that Tracey felt she could not challenge, but few hold sympathy with that view.

This was more than a blind eye turned. When asked by doctors and social workers to explain Peter's injuries, his mother said variously that he fell because he was such a boisterous character, that he'd slipped and hit his head on a fireplace, that it must have happened when he was in his grandmother's care, that he'd got into fights with other children and of course, when words weren't enough, the lasting image of Peter smeared in chocolate remains with the public for ever.

She covered his cuts and bruises with melted chocolate, a shocking parody of the kind of life a seventeen-month-old baby should have been leading, exploring food whilst an indulgent mother looked on.

Why would any mother act this way? Again, it is vital to push past the despair such cases generate to understand and hopefully begin to prevent such cruelty destroying the lives of other infants. Peter had not always been subjected to brutality; in fact, when he was born his path seemed to be mapped out very differently. He was born on 1 March 2006 at the North Middlesex Hospital in London and he was not his mother and father's first child. Tracey had married Peter's father in 2003 and at that point, they already had two daughters. A third would follow. Peter was their fourth child and to the outside world he was a blessing.

The proud parents returned to their home in Haringey but any hopes for their future together were short-lived. From the outside, this seemed like a stable family but it was not the case. Tracey had experienced post-natal depression before and it seemed that Peter's arrival would trigger another collapse into depression. But more than the hardships that the condition brings, there was a deeper unhappiness in the marriage. Tracey was only sixteen when she met her future husband, who was considerably older at thirty-three, yet she had fallen for the man who seemed to promise much that had been missing in her formative years – a stable father figure.

Tracey was born not in London but in the Midlands to an Irish mother who was married to a man who may or may not be Tracey's father. Her mother had a fraught and impoverished background: her own mother had died shortly after childbirth and she lost her stepmother by the time she was five. When Tracey's mother arrived in England, she was already scarred from a life of violence and abuse. She quickly married, divorced and was married again, this time to a man who beat her. The couple had a son and they broke up some years later when Tracey was almost the same age Peter was when he met his brutal death. When Tracey was eighteen months old, her mother moved to London with her daughter but not her son. He arrived in London some years later after his father passed away but his mother struggled to care for him and social services became involved.

Tracey came to the attention of social services too. Her home life was difficult and it worsened when her mother told her that her father was not her real dad after all. It was a revelation that she found hard to cope with and she later stated in court that 'It sent me a bit wild for a while'. Perhaps that was an understatement – she was a young girl profoundly unhappy with her life and in danger of heading into a life of drugs misuse and delinquency. When Tracey was twelve years old, social services arranged for her to attend a boarding school, believing that a stable environment might help her overcome her problems.

Removing a child from a troubled home life is never a decision lightly faced. If a home is proving detrimental to a child's physical and emotional well-being then options have to be explored and a boarding school can offer some children a route out of a damaging childhood. But for some the opportunities a boarding school presents do not cancel out a sense of abandonment and a fear of authority. Even well-meaning agencies such as social services can be viewed with hostility as this was the department that tore a family apart. It is not without contradictions but it is often how the human heart feels; instead of feeling resentment towards a mother and father who failed to provide a loving and stable home, it is the agencies that brought about change that face the anger of an abused child.

Tracey learnt a great deal about social services in her dealings with them. She learnt that they can wield great power but also that they have a language and culture that you can learn to navigate, rather than swim against. Social services are staffed with people who dedicate themselves to improving the lot of the disadvantaged and hope that their intervention will lead to a better outcome for the families they support. Child protection is a very difficult and emotionally exhausting job. Caseworkers are threatened, some seriously assaulted and few are unaffected by the day-to-day stresses they face. Inevitably, they respond to certain markers when they talk to clients – it would be impossible not to. A mother from a disadvantaged home who responds to questions not with hostility and threats but says, 'I want to be a brilliant mother', will be listened to sympathetically. Showing a willingness to cooperate and an understanding that support and advice can help improve her children's environment is to be welcomed. Tracey told her caseworker: 'I want to be a brilliant mother.'

Outwardly, she cooperated with social services. She kept her appointments, she continued to take her son to visit GPs' surgeries and sought help when he had stomach upsets. She also took part in an assessment project, a study using Solution Focused Brief Therapy. Developed in America, the therapy asks clients to talk about their hopes for the future and in doing so, try to find methods to tackle current difficulties and past problems. Tracey agreed to take part in a social worker's study as she was working towards a qualification in the technique. She was filmed talking about her life and her hopes for the future, she talked with confidence and painted a picture that was far removed from the realities of her life in Haringey.

She was sufficiently familiar with caseworkers and procedure to be seen to cooperate and in doing so, Peter's fate was almost certainly sealed. Had she been dysfunctional and uncooperative, the child protection team may well have insisted that Peter be removed from her care. As it was, he was allowed to remain in the house and was exposed to Steven Barker.

The fact that Barker was 'hidden' has been well covered although there is a dispute about how truly hidden he was. Without doubt, had his presence been clearly documented he would have been subject to background checks, just as the boyfriend of Claire Biggs would have. It is easy to lie, easy to clear out belongings of a live-in lover before careworkers arrive at a property and easy to deny that anyone other than the mother has access to a child. If Tracey was saying one thing to social workers, she was saying something quite different online. There, in the chat rooms she visited, she talked of how happy she was with her handsome and strapping new boyfriend, again, painting a picture that was at odds with the truth.

Tracey had met Barker in 2004 when she was visiting a friend and he was fixing something at their house. He was an odd-job man working for an agency that repaired tenants' properties. Barker was markedly different from her husband: young, blond, well-built and standing over six foot three, Tracey was soon drawn to him. Her husband became aware of the friendship and it put yet more strain on the marriage. After Peter was born, Tracey began to receive counselling for depression once more but within three months, her marriage was at an end.

The final blow came when Tracey suggested that she wanted to take her 'friend', not her husband, to a school reunion. He moved out in July 2006 and it is unclear when Barker moved in – it was certainly by the end of the year and in October, Peter was taken on one of many visits to a GP who noted bruising to his head and chest. Tracey said that the eight-month-old baby had fallen down the stairs. In December he was back again, this time with injuries to his head, the bridge of his nose, his sternum, right shoulder and buttocks. The GP referred Peter to Whittington Hospital and as the mother's explanation for her son's injuries was less than convincing, the paediatrician called social services.

Peter was placed in temporary care and the police called at the house. Peter's sisters showed no visible signs of injury. Peter was then looked after by a registered childminder for six weeks over the Christmas period of 2006 and physically he seemed to thrive, gaining weight and with no more unexplained bruising appearing. The childminder did note, however, that Peter would headbutt and bite. Sadly, the psychological impact of the violence he had been subjected to seemed to have profoundly unsettled him.

Peter's old home was a mess. As part of the plan to help the family function once more, the decision was made to relocate them to Tottenham and into a new four-bedroom house. It was a home that Barker intended to move into as well and it would be the property that would prove deadly for baby Peter.

Social services were still unaware that the boyfriend was living under the same roof and they were also unaware that a new lodger was about to move in with a large contingent of his own. Professionals came and went, the shortest period that the house was not visited was only ten days, and yet the charade went on. Peter would be seen covered with yet more injuries, he would be examined, he would be assessed and then he would be returned. It is easy to dismiss the efforts of the social care team but in truth, they saw Peter headbutt family members, saw him fall and not cry and it seemed to support his mother's claim that he was a boisterous child with a high pain threshold.

His sisters attended school regularly, seemed injury-free and the mother cooperated. The prime concern seemed to be one of support, to help Tracey who had a history of depression and who complained of ongoing fatigue. The house was unkempt at best, it smelt and was littered with mess – clearly Tracey could not cope with the day-to-day demands of parenting. It did not register with any of the professionals that someone else was orchestrating an ongoing campaign of physical abuse and terror. Peter could not tell them. His mother stayed silent.

At some point in June 2007, Barker's brother Jason Owen moved in. By that point, Tracey had been interviewed under caution by police in connection with some of her son's injuries. Owen, then 35 years old, was not alone. He arrived with his fifteen-year-old girlfriend and five other children aged from fourteen to seven, a dog and a pet snake. Tracey is said to have complained to friends and said that Owen had refused to leave. Clearly, it was OK with Barker that Owen had arrived and Tracey said she felt afraid of Owen but, once again, she voiced no concern to her social workers or the police.

It will never be known what took place in the final few days of Peter's life. By the time Owen moved in, Peter had but a few weeks to live. His head was shaved, Tracey said to help rid him of head lice, and the numerous cuts on his head became infected and clearly visible. Again, it should be stressed that Tracey took him to GPs' surgeries repeatedly, she was not hiding her son away, and she picked up several prescriptions for courses of antibiotics. It is a contradiction that is difficult to understand; she was treating the symptoms whilst allowing him to be exposed to the cruel source of all his ills.

It would be easy to dismiss her gestures as part of a cynical cover up but perhaps it hints at a far more disturbing truth. In the course of her dealing with female offenders, Anna Motz has identified that disturbed women fail to see their child as separate from themselves, he or she is an extension of themselves and a depository for ill-feeling. Women who have had poor experiences of being mothered themselves frequently struggle when they come to have children. Some idealise what a child will mean, believing that a baby will 'love them' and be pure and good. When the infant cries and is inconsolable, it can both mirror what the mother felt as a child and underline their sense of self as 'no good'. As Motz writes: 'She has powerfully identified with the helplessness of the child, and has found her inability to provide for the needs of the infant intolerable. The identification is so painful and so unbearable that the situation cannot be allowed to continue.' The result can be catastrophic.

Tracey spoke in glowing terms about her boyfriend, a man with a naked obsession with Nazi memorabilia and a fascination with pain. In blotting out his actual character she was inventing a fantasy, painting a picture of a man who made her feel good, who cared for her and wanted her – all qualities missing from her early childhood. It was a dangerous cocktail of need, denial and fantasy. In neglecting Peter, she was neglecting herself, the 'bad things' that if her boyfriend did not want, she did not want. The boy was a symbol of the past, her past life, her past marriage. If her boyfriend wanted to 'destroy' that, she allowed it to happen.

Set against that was the see-sawing of taking Peter to be examined by medical professionals – she wanted them to help Peter as it seemed to be beyond her abilities to make him well. Again, she was pushing her responsibilities onto another agency, avoiding what needed to be faced. As no one stepped in and stopped the horror, Peter's mother merely accepted that this is how things would continue. She imagined she'd tried then sank back into hours on the sofa, complaining of illness, interspersed with hours online, elaborating on how this man in her life 'made her feel special'.

What motivated Barker's sadism can only be guessed at but it would come as little surprise to forensic psychologists if they were to learn that he came from a severely abusive background, beginning when he himself was Peter's age. The link between childhood experience and adult behaviour is seen in violent offenders time and time again. It does in no way excuse the behaviour but is invaluable when exploring how and why such extreme brutality can emerge. Lloyd deMause is an American social thinker who has written about what motivates those who abuse children and says: 'It involves using the child as what I have termed a "poison container", a receptacle into which one can project disowned parts of one's psyche, so that one can manipulate and control these feelings in another body without danger to one's self'.

Tragically for Peter, his tiny body was the receptacle for his mother's sense of neglect and worthlessness and her boyfriend's outbursts of sadistic terror. One boy was the rag being pulled between two damaged individuals in a deeply dysfunctional relationship.

On 3 August 2007, the London Ambulance Service received a call to attend a house in Tottenham – a child had stopped breathing. When the paramedics reached the home, they found Peter's mother crouched over him in the tiny and filthy bedroom. They tried to resuscitate the toddler but he was already blue and stiff to the touch, wearing only a nappy. The two paramedics told Tracey that they would take him to North Middlesex Hospital, the very place he was born only seventeen months earlier. She asked them to wait whilst she found her cigarettes.

All attempts to revive Peter failed and the police were called. Tracey was arrested and taken to Edmonton police station. In the meantime, officers travelled to her home where they found Barker. He said he was only visiting the house but he was arrested. It took some time before he admitted that he had a sexual relationship with Tracey and that he was the father of the child she was now expecting – she was three months pregnant.

At some point, Peter's bedding was removed and disposed of. Whatever had gone on in the household, some of those involved were attempting to cover up what had happened to the little boy. Jason Owen was arrested too and the police knew they would face an uphill struggle to secure a murder verdict for the simple reason that it was not clear who of the three had carried out the final act of brutality that extinguished Peter's life. In November 2008, Jason Owen and Steven Barker were found guilty of causing Peter's death; Tracey pleaded guilty to the same charge.

When the story hit the news public outrage was instantaneous. Further terrible events at the home were yet to follow as police have also investigated the rape of a girl, then aged two years old, by Barker. The identities of the two adults at that point had to remain secret as this separate trial had to be carried out without the risk of prejudicing a jury. On 1 May 2009, the jury found Barker guilty of rape but Tracey was cleared of causing or allowing the abuse of the girl.

Later that same month, they were back in court for sentencing. Barker received a sentence of twelve years for causing Peter's death and a life sentence for raping a two-year-old girl. He must serve at least ten years. Initially, Jason Owen was given an indeterminate sentence for causing Peter's death but after a successful appeal in 2009, it was replaced with a sentence of six years. Tracey Connelly was told that she would be jailed indefinitely for causing or allowing her son's death and will serve a minimum of five years.

She had sent a letter to the judge in advance of arriving at court to hear her sentence. She wrote: 'I except (sic) I failed my son Peter for which I have pleaded guilty. By not being fully open with the social workers I stopped them from being able to do a full job, as a direct result of this my son got hurt and sadly lost his short life.' She went on to write of her life being filled with guilt as she struggles to come to terms with her 'failure as a mother'.

In the eyes of most, this failure to be a mother is the hardest thing of all to accept. We demand that women put their children's lives before their own and even though the majority of mothers do so without hesitation, there is a harder truth to be faced – some women do not have the capacity to mother and demanding that they should will never be enough to save the lives of children like Peter.

When the 999 call was finally made, the boyfriend told the mother to lie about how the baby was found. She had done nothing about the scores of cuts and bruises on her child, not even when the toddler cried as its bones were broken – why would she not do as she was told this time, now that they were both in serous trouble as they looked down on the lifeless body at their feet? This wasn't Peter, this was Sanam Navsarka, born in the same year as Peter and slowly beaten to death by 21-year-old Subhan Anwar, her mother's boyfriend. The mother, Zahbeena Navsarka, also twenty-one, was jailed for nine years for her daughter's manslaughter, and Anwar was jailed for life.

The judge, Peter Thornton, told Zahbeena: 'Your deliberate cruelty is beyond belief ... You put your relationship with Anwar first, ignoring the needs of your vulnerable child. You failed to protect her from serious harm, knowing what was being done to her.' Police had found tiny handprints and bloodstains inside the cupboard that Sanam had been locked in at her mother's home in Huddersfield. Another infant unable to talk about her torment, another mother failing her child, another boyfriend drawing out his hideous impulses on a defenceless child.

It is happening now, somewhere, a mother's neglect proving more aggressive and dangerous than any smack, a child unable to find shelter. Kids Company founder Camila Batmanghelidjh believes that in the inner city areas where she works, up to one in five children are being neglected. Other studies estimate that as many as half of under-resourced mothers living in deprived areas with young children in the UK will suffer from clinical depression. The numbers are staggering and within them will be those too dysfunctional to prevent their children being subject to abuse.

Being a mother is not enough; it has to be accepted that some women will abuse those in their care. Perhaps the notion that women cannot be abusers has been ended once and for all with the conviction of Vanessa George and Angela Allen for their involvement in the horrific sexual abuse of children.

The NSPCC is right to run its 'Full Stop' campaign, demanding that cruelty to children must stop. It is also one of a number of organisations that run research into why it occurs and, as a society, we owe it to children to see beyond our moral outrage. We need to find more effective ways to identify those at risk, to prevent the abused growing into adults who perpetuate abuse on the next generation, and we need to provide those removed into care with meaningful and enriched lives.

We don't want to read any more headlines about the torture of children. We don't want to read statements such as that made by Peter's father who wrote: 'Like all fathers I had imagined watching my son grow up, playing football with him, taking him to see Arsenal play, watching him open his Christmas and birthday presents and just develop as a person. All of that has been taken from me.'

Never again do we want to read about toddlers like Rhys, Peter and Sanam being hunted and killed in their own homes but it remains to be seen if we, as a society, can find ways to prevent cycles of abuse and neglect claiming life after life.